Sources for the History of Cyprus

Edited by
Paul W. Wallace and Andreas G. Orphanides

Volume IV
Pero Tafur and Cyprus

Essay, Translation, and Commentaries by
Colbert I. Nepaulsingh
(University at Albany, State University of New York)

Greece and Cyprus Research Center
1997

Copyright 1997 by Greece and Cyprus Research Center, Inc.
Altamont, New York 12009

ISBN: 0-9651704-4-6

ISBN set: 0-9651704-0-3

Sources for the History of Cyprus

Volume IV

Pero Tafur and Cyprus

This study is dedicated to

Vice President David W. Martin

and

Dean Paul W. Wallace

and

Professor James B. Larkin

TABLE OF CONTENTS

I. INTRODUCTION 1

II. TEXTS AND CONTEXTS 9

    Passage 1: Tafur tells about the Genoese at Famagusta
                 and about the Mala Paga prison 9
    Passage 2: Tafur stops at Cyprus en route to Jerusalem 9
    Passage 3: Tafur returns to Cyprus for permission to visit
                 Mount Sinai 10
    Passage 4: The King of Cyprus sends Tafur on a mission
                 to the Sultan of Egypt 11
    Passage 5: Tafur mentions Cyprus to Niccolo Conti 18
    Passage 6: Tafur returns the Sultan's reply to Cyprus 19
    Passage 7: Tafur mentions how Cypriots live in Venice 22

III. APPENDICES 23

    Appendix 1: Larkin's Transcript of the Cyprus Passages 23
    Appendix 2: Monstrelet on the capture of King Janus of Cyprus 43
    Appendix 3: Johnes's English translation of Monstrelet 48

IV. NOTES 53

    BIBLIOGRAPHY 62
    INDEX 66

I. INTRODUCTION

Previous attempts to fix correctly the beginning of Pero Tafur's adventures and travels have not been conclusive. This essay establishes, for the first time, that on May 17, 1436, according to his own words, Pero Tafur set out in his native Spain to travel to Jerusalem.[1] His journey lasted three years and took him to many cities around the Mediterranean Sea before he returned to Spain in the Spring of 1439. During this journey, Tafur stopped twice on Cyprus and performed two missions for the king of that island, John II: one to the Sultan of Egypt, and the other to the Grand Master of the Order of Rhodes. These missions, though minor, are part of the long and fascinating history of Cyprus, and it is no surprise that the major historians of the island use Tafur's account as an authoritative source.

These historians often rely on the only complete English translation of Tafur's account, the one published by Malcolm Letts in 1926 under the title *Pero Tafur, Travels and Adventures 1435-1439*.[2] Letts's translation is more than adequate for the casual reader of travelogues, but for scholarly purposes it is unreliable for two main reasons. First, Letts almost always improves Tafur's awkward prose, making his translation a copy-edited version rather than an accurate rendition into English of what Tafur wrote. More significantly, for the purposes of accurate scholarship, Letts's translation is too often wrong. Let two examples dealing with Cyprus suffice here where there are many. Letts claims that, shortly after receiving and answering letters from the King of Cyprus, the Grand Master of the Order of Rhodes died of a liver ailment: *When I arrived I found the Master grievously ill with a pain in his liver, but he soon dispatched the answers to the King of Cyprus, and I took my leave and returned to my lodging. That night he died of his sickness* (107). In fact, Tafur wrote that the Grand Master had a pain *in his side* (126), and Letts is simply confusing the Spanish word for side (*ijada*) with the word for liver (*higado*). On another occasion, Letts claims that Tafur met the Cardinal of Cyprus in Venice and toured the city with him: *He was about to depart for Cyprus, the galley which was to take him being moored to the door of his house, and there I met him and went with him through the city* (167). In fact, Tafur is describing here the marvel that in Venice wealthy people can board their huge ships at their doorstep, and he says that the Cardinal's galley, not Tafur, met the Cardinal at his doorstep, and the same galley took the Cardinal through the middle of the city. Tafur saw the Cardinal leave Venice for Cyprus, on that occasion, but did not leave with him. These might well be insignificant details for the casual reader, but for the scholar, it makes a big difference whether or not one dies of a liver ailment or accompanies someone important on a boat headed for Cyprus.

For these reasons, the seven passages about Cyprus from Tafur's account, arranged in this study under **Texts and Contexts,** do not attempt to improve his loose prose to make interesting reading for travel lovers. Where it is necessary to add words in English that do not have an equivalent in Tafur's Spanish, the added words are placed in square brackets. Wherever an English word can be found that matches Tafur's Spanish etymologically without unduly distorting the meaning of the original, that word is preferred, even if the result in English sounds stilted. In order to give the reader an appreciation of the full context in which Tafur talks about Cyprus, I summarize, very briefly, those portions of the narrative that do not mention Cyprus. The summaries are in normal type; the translations of Tafur's text dealing with Cyprus are in italics. The titles for all seven passages are coined for the reader's convenience by the author of this essay, not by Tafur.

The autograph of Tafur's text is lost and has survived in only one known copy done in the eighteenth century, MS M-1985 of the University of Salamanca Library. For these summaries and translations, therefore, I have relied on the notes for a paleographic edition (of the unique manuscript) being prepared by Professor James B. Larkin, checking those notes against the edition by Marcos Jiménez de la Espada, published in Madrid in 1874 and reprinted recently in 1982; I refer always to the 1874 edition.

The manuscript has ninety-one folios and only eight small gaps, two in the prologue on the first folio, one on the last page, and five scattered at random throughout the manuscript. Jiménez marks these gaps in his edition (at pages 1, 2, 43, 47, 108, 112, 139, 169, 302), and he informs us, overconfidently in the light of the missing original, that the eighteenth-century copy is quite faithful to the orthography, punctuation, and language of the fifteenth century, which is why he deems the copy authentic (xxi). Larkin assures us (4–5) that "the entire MS is in excellent condition with nothing missing. The lacunae that occur in the text undoubtedly reflect the imperfect state of the original; omissions are clearly indicated by blanks (not by 'series de puntos' as Jiménez claims)." For his part, Jiménez says that he regularizes the orthography without changing its fifteenth-century character, corrects obvious minor errors "having to do with articles, prepositions, conjunctions, etc." without noting the many times he does so; and, on the other hand, he indicates where he has added words or lines not in the copy he is using (xxiv). It is regrettable that Jiménez did not aim to produce a critical edition and that those who reprinted his text in 1982 have repeated his minor errors in facsimile. As Larkin points out, Jiménez's "norms of spelling are neither clear nor are they uniformly applied; in addition, there are instances of gratuitous 'correction' not justified by the internal grammatical evidence of the text" (5). For these reasons also, the appendix of this study includes Professor Larkin's paleographic transcription of the passages dealing with Cyprus.

Jiménez was aware that Tafur's manuscript has reached us not in chapters but in very uneven paragraphs, and although he notes the "disorderly shape" of these paragraphs (xv), Jiménez is careful to leave these divisions as he found them. In the manuscript, paragraph breaks are indicated by a blank line, as Professor Larkin has confirmed to me. Letts, on the other hand, rearranges the manuscript's thirty-nine paragraphs into twenty-nine chapters, and he divides the long paragraphs, some of which run on for many pages, into shorter ones. This makes for easy twentieth-century reading, but, again, it distorts the logic of the divisions of the manuscript as it has reached us. It will always be a matter of conjecture, in the absence of the original, whether these paragraph divisions were intended by Tafur or imposed upon his original during its transmission. It is therefore important to maintain the integrity of the unique manuscript's paragraph divisions, so that scholars might make educated guesses, if they so choose, about the shape of Tafur's original. Only on thirteen out of a possible thirty-eight occasions does Letts follow the manuscript's paragraph divisions.

Tafur's paragraphs, although they range in length from a few lines to as many as forty-eight pages, are arranged in three long cores with their satellites, in accordance with the respective bases of operation for a three-legged journey to the lands of the Sultan of Egypt, the lands of the Turks, and the Christian lands of Europe. The first such core is Cyprus, and it is the base of operations for the journey to the lands of the Sultan of Egypt. In this first leg of the journey, Tafur does visit Venice, but, significantly, he does not describe it: at this stage of the narrative, Venice is a necessary stopover for Jerusalem and the lands of the Sultan. On the other hand, all the passages dealing with Cyprus, except the last minor passage, are found in this first of three portions of Tafur's narrative between the prologue and the end of paragraph 14. Tafur's choice makes historical sense because Cyprus was an important symbol in Christendom, and the monarch of Cyprus was also crowned King or Queen of Jerusalem.

The second core of paragraphs deals with Constantinople, base of operations for Tafur's visit to the Turkish lands, and this core and its satellites comprise paragraphs 15 through 24. Venice is the core of the third portion of the narrative and the base of Tafur's visit to the Christian lands of Europe (paragraphs 25 through 39).

Just as scholars need to know the shape in which Tafur's narrative has been transmitted, it is equally important to understand why he claims to have written it, and what contemporary context may have incited him to do so. Tafur explains his motive clearly in the prologue to his narrative.

According to the prologue, Tafur's narrative is not meant merely as a travelogue for a pilgrimage to Jerusalem and a journey throughout Europe but rather as a *treatise* (1, 2) on good government. Good government, according to the prologue, is government by the nobility, and *one can be called noble for as long as he follows the customs of others* [who were] *his ancestors* (1). In Tafur's opinion, virtuous nobles should travel to other lands and perform deeds of prowess even before their identity is revealed, in order to demonstrate who their ancestors were. And, upon returning home, noble knights should report the styles of government they encountered so that their country can be better governed (2). This, precisely, is what Tafur claims to have done.

Cyprus, the first core of Tafur's narrative, was, regrettably, at that time, an example of the worst kind of government, in Tafur's schema, because part of it (Famagusta) was misruled by Genoa, and because all of it paid tribute to the Sultan of Egypt. About Genoa, Tafur writes, *this city, for all its patrimony, has community rule* (12–13); and Egypt, for Tafur, was a place where slaves, mamelukes, ruled. Constantinople, the second core, was also an example of bad government, in Tafur's hierarchy, because there an Emperor was persuaded to treat commoners and the nobility as equals, which led to civil war until Pedro Yllan, the person Tafur claimed to be his ancestor, restored the superiority of the nobles (141–148). Venice, the third core country in Tafur's narrative, like Florence, was an example of good government. In Venice, noblemen were hanged separately from commoners, and *the Venetians have as law not to choose a Duke nor give a government position* [to anyone] *unless he is a nobleman by birth, and* [the position is] *in perpetuity, unless he does something to make them take it away from him; and every Sunday, after eating, ... all the noblemen come, and there they notify them of all that was done the past week, in government as well as in civil and criminal justice, everything, except the secret council, especially pertaining to war, which is held with the deputies and the Duke* (208). In Venice there was even a good Duke who refused to be King (212).

To make certain that we understand the hierarchy of government, Tafur made an example of Pisa, on one bad extreme, and Florence, excellent at the other extreme. Pisa was then owned by Florence, Tafur explains, because Pisans *made their* [few remaining] *nobles fall down low, and they even say that, for dishonor, they make them wear their berets in reverse, and they are the scorn of the people and subjects of those who were their slaves* (294–95). Florence, on the other hand, *is ruled for months by singular persons, by lot on whomever it falls, and perhaps it might befall the shoemaker as well as the knight, but its government cannot be improved...* [and in their] *hospitals, the best in the world, ... each person is given a spot according to his condition, but the care for all is equal; what will people so discreet do that is not good?* (292–93). Good government for Tafur, therefore, is discreet government. Where the nobility is in control, a discreet carpenter can rule as well as a knight. Where nobility is not maintained, war ensues, as in Germany where the seventy-five-year-old Empress left her husband to marry the twelve-year-old King of Poland, and it took the discreet Bishop of Burgos, in Tafur's narrative, to restore peace (275–76).

There is some evidence that Tafur took notes as he travelled: he copied verbatim the inscriptions on the tombs of Godfrey of Bouillon and his brother Baldwin in Jerusalem (56). And many passages have an immediacy that is attributable either to an impeccable memory after a long period of time or, what is more likely, to notes taken shortly after the event. Moreover, Tafur realized the value of carrying detailed news from one country and its leaders to another, and he would have known that his reputation would be tarnished if his memory was not aided by careful notes. And yet, although these notes were probably written between 1436 and 1439, we know that Tafur did not finish the narrative before 1454, fifteen years after he returned to Spain. What was happening in Spain around 1454 that would have forced Tafur to polish his travel notes as a treatise on good government and send it to a powerful nobleman, the Master of the Order of Calatrava?

In Spain around 1454, two events closely related to Tafur's travels must have forced him to pick up his travel notes. Constantinople, the place Tafur claims as the home of his noble ancestors, fell to the Turks in 1453, and the King of Castile, who provided Tafur with letters of recommendation for his journey, died in 1454; in his revised treatise, Tafur includes both of these events as having recently occurred. They must have shaken Tafur terribly. One of the major purposes of his journey, he states, was to notice military matters so as to help his king govern well and defeat the Moors. In Cyprus, he had watched a king cornered in a fortress and made to capitulate to the demands of his subjects. In Egypt, he paid careful attention to the military salute paid to the Sultan. In Constantinople, he had watched for days as the Turkish army passed perilously close. In Venice, he took careful notes as galleys were outfitted on a medieval assembly line. In Milan, he studied the Duke's army and noted how weapons were manufactured. And now, Constantinople had fallen, and the king who had recommended his journey had died. This is most likely why Tafur wrote in his prologue that the *times* [are] *not a little clouded* (2).

The times were clouded then in Spain not just because Constantinople had fallen and the king of Castile had died, but especially because Spain itself was in a state of terrible turmoil. Since 1391, around the time that Tafur might have been born, good government, in the sense Tafur understood it, had gone awry: the people he considered commoners, the "little people," had toppled the ones he called noble.

> When King John I of Castile died in 1390, the crown prince was still a minor. The regency which administered the government in behalf of the boy-king was not strong enough to hold the various rebellious forces in check... [In Seville] the synagogues were converted into churches and the Jewish quarter was settled by Christians within a short time. The storm that broke in Seville passed over all the other communities of Andalusia, and extended to New and Old Castile... The famous synagogues of Toledo fell into Christian hands, and some were destroyed... In Madrid most of the Jews were killed or baptized. The municipal authorities cast all the blame upon the "little people" (*pueblo menudo*), who continued to loot in the vicinity for a whole year (Baer 2:96–97).

Jews in Spain, therefore, around the time that Tafur was born, faced either with forced conversion to Catholicism or death, left Spain for all the lands Tafur visited later from 1436 to 1439. There is perhaps no better explanation for the fact that Tafur meets Castilians in almost every country he visits. Palestine, Constantinople, and Venice were especially favored points of destination for large numbers of Jews and conversos from Spain after 1391. "Emigration to Palestine, which in thirteenth-and-fourteenth century Spain had been a matter for the select few, now became a great mass movement" (Baer 2: 158). Venice was known to be less hostile to Jews than most other European cities at that time. And in Constantinople, Jews were often accused of selling European secrets to the Turks.

From 1391 to the expulsion of the Jews in 1492, the situation in Spain worsened, especially for conversos. Whether these conversos were sincere Christians or secret Judaizers, they were considered New (hence inferior) Christians, and their quick entry into the mainstream of Castilian life made them targets of intense hatred from ignoble Old Christians. Tafur's narrative portrays him as a sincere Old Christian who can trace his lineage back to the Christian Emperor of Constantinople, but the idea cannot be dismissed that his text depicts the agonies of a New Christian in Spain in the first half of the fifteenth century. This is not the place to treat the matter in detail, but analysis of Tafur's religious status in Spain should include the following facts, which are not intended to be definitive proof of anything, but which, cumulatively, invite further investigation.

Tafur allows the Chief Interpreter of the Sultan of Egypt, a Jew from Seville, to believe that he Tafur *was of his nation* (78), a phrase in which the word *nation* is carefully chosen to mean either country or tribe or both; here, Tafur's discreet empathy with whomever he is speaking comes into play, as it does, for example, when he tells Niccolo Conti that he was from Italy but raised in Cyprus (95), or when he told poor knights who tried to rob him that he too was a poor knight (281), or when, in order to empathize with the Count Urbino, he disguised himself as a poor pious beggar from Rome on a pilgrimage to Jerusalem (38). But there is also some truth in each of these discreet attempts at empathy, leaving us to wonder whether the truth lies in his being from Seville or in his being Jewish.

Again, several of Tafur's contacts outside of Spain have surnames (like Caro, Quexada, Torquemada) that figure prominently in Jewish history as well as in the records of the Spanish Inquisition. The bishop of Burgos, Alonso de Cartagena, who treated Tafur as a friend and reported back to the King of Castile about Tafur's loyal behavior at the Council of Basle, was a famous converso to Christianity from Judaism (277–278). When Tafur described his visit to the Red Sea, he explained the folklore concerning the island of Susan *from where*, he writes, *they say that the Jews come whom in Castile they call abensusenes* (98). In Rome, Tafur visited the ancient Jewish quarter (27). And it might be no accident that he preferred how Venetians govern, since Venice at that time was known throughout Europe for accommodating Jews.

Tafur insisted on visiting Mount Sinai (which is what necessitates his trip to Cyprus, as we shall see), and he came away with *the emblem of Saint Catherine, which is the wheel of the knives of gold*; I have argued elsewhere that Saint Catherine's wheel of torture had become in Spain a symbol of the misfortune of the conversos (Nepaulsingh 1987, 200).

Documents in Córdoba show that Tafur married a woman, Juana de Horozco, with a surname found with some regularity among Spanish Jews, and that Tafur's sister married a man with a Jewish surname, Fernán Mexía; another document from Córdoba dated July 20, 1479, shows Tafur, as alderman, receiving a commission from the city to "secure sites for building mosques and synagogues for Jews and Moors" (Ramírez de Arellano 282, 283, 287).

Increasingly from 1391, there was intense pressure throughout Spain to prohibit conversos from holding public office. Finally in 1473, "the municipal council of Córdoba passed an ordinance to exclude *conversos* from posts in the municipality" (Baer 2:308). If he were converso, Tafur would have sensed the building pressure for such an ordinance for many years, and he would have been encouraged to demonstrate his Old Christian heritage with a book like his *Andanças*; and yet, in that book, his description of forced conversion in Egypt invites unmistakable comparison with forced conversion in Spain (see note 18 below). There can be no doubt that the main purpose of Tafur's book is to demonstrate his lineage. The section on Constantinople which links Tafur to the Emperor via Pedro Yllan is at the very center, the heart of the narrative.

But the attempt itself, and the repetitive nature of the claim to Old Christian heritage, reflect the concerns of the author of the autobiographical text. Why would a noble Christian of such old standing have to go to such persistent lengths to prove his heritage, especially at a time when many conversos were known to be in the process of inventing their lineage in order to survive? What is more, while there are documents that link the Byzantine name Yllan (Julian) with Spain long before Tafur's time, Tafur's narrative is the first known document to link the name Tafur with the name Yllan; and Tafur admits that the connection is fuzzy because of marriages over the years (146). In addition, the cleverness of the choice of name, Yllan or Julian, with which to link the name Tafur is overbearing. It is common knowledge that Count Julian was the Byzantine governor of the city of Ceuta who, with the help of many Spanish Jews, assisted the Arabs in conquering Spain in the year 711. The Arab point of entry in 711 was Gibraltar, which is precisely where Tafur chooses to begin his narrative with another defeat of the Christian Spaniards at the hands of the Arabs in 1436.

Perhaps the most telling piece of textual evidence of Tafur's ancestry is the possibility that, like other converso writers of Jewish descent, Tafur inserts his name into his text in an artistically defiant way. Knowing that the word *tahur* has a pejorative denotation in Spanish, Tafur uses it in a clearly laudatory context, leaving the distinct impression that he may have known that in Biblical Hebrew the word *tahur* means the very opposite of what it came to mean in Spanish (see below, note 23, and Nepaulsingh 1995, 52, 53, 55, 120).

Looked at in this way, Tafur's narrative seems like a series of anguished attempts to prove his loyalty to Castile, to Christianity, and to chivalry, in the face of what he considers the patent disloyalty of several of the characters he describes. If Jews helped Count Julian and the Arabs at Gibraltar in 711, Tafur, even though he is sick and otherwise unprepared for the fight, helps Count Niebla against the Arabs at Gibraltar in 1436 (3–5). If a Jew from Seville helps the Sultan of Egypt exact tribute from the Christian King of Cyprus, Tafur helps that King relieve himself from the Sultan's taxes (83). If Castilians abroad, like Mosen Suárez in Cyprus, yield to the temptation of serving the leaders of other countries for personal gain, Tafur steadfastly refuses all such offers in order that he might return as soon as possible to help the king of Castile, Juan II. If the emperors of Constantinople have forgotten their loyalty to their original coat of arms, Tafur reminds them of it and of its relationship to Castile (149). If enemies of the Christian faith enslave Christians, Tafur risks his life to free Christian slaves (186), and, with the Pope's blessing, he buys slaves at Kaffa to save them from apostasy (162). If some Christians in Europe, like the Bohemian Hussites, have fallen prey to heresy, Tafur is careful to denounce the dangers inherent in that heresy (270–71).

Loyalty, in the sense of intense devotion and a desire to please and conform, is a theme that Tafur establishes even in the prologue to his narrative when he sends it to his patron *especially considering the great devotion the person sending it has had and will have to please* [the patron] *always* (1). Tafur holds up, as a model of loyalty, the Castilian Pedro de la Randa who refuses to renounce his Christian faith even in the face of death, tricks his Catalan counterpart into dying rather than apostatizing, and eventually dies insisting on fighting the Moors and not the Christians (112–116). Pedro de la Randa's famous story is meant by Tafur to be contrasted with the stories of Niccolo de Conti and the Emperor of Trebizond whose marriages complicate their loyalty to Christianity (96, 97, 160).

Although he mentions the fall of Constantinople in 1453 and the death of King John II in 1454, it is curious that Tafur makes no direct mention in his narrative of the execution on June 2, 1453, of the powerful Constable of Castile, Alvaro de Luna. Indeed, it can be argued that Tafur's declarations of loyalty to the king, coupled with his silence about Alvaro de Luna, are indications that he sided with those who fought to overthrow Alvaro de Luna. No prominent Castilian who, like Tafur, had dealings with the king's court from 1419 to 1453 would have been unaware of the battle between Alvaro de Luna and his adversaries for access to the king. When the king was about five years old, Alvaro, who was then about twenty one, became the king's page. The king had no closer friend and adviser until he turned against Alvaro and ordered his execution in 1453.

In the light of Tafur's emphasis on a type of good government that favors the nobility against commoners, Tafur's narrative might be interpreted as an anti-Luna document. With respect to this interpretation, it can be noted that Alvaro de Luna was the illegitimate son of a nobleman and a commoner. Alvaro's adversaries accused him of appointing too many commoners, especially Jews and New Christians, to the king's government and of using his position as the king's *privado* (plenipotent private secretary) to usurp the king's powers. Some enemies even went so far as to accuse Alvaro of homosexually perverting the young king (Round 8, 25). Tafur dedicates his narrative to a leader of the Order of Calatrava, an institution that was not likely to support Alvaro de Luna's appointment of commoners at its expense. Also, as Professor Larkin has reminded me (in private correspondence), the episode in which Tafur describes the downfall of the King of Cyprus's *privado* (120–121) would have been read by Castilians in comparison with the downfall of Alvaro de Luna in 1453; the comparison would have been almost inevitable because Tafur takes care to mention that the Cypriot *privado*, Jacobo Guiri, had made a visit to Castile (70). Finally, when Tafur makes a gratuitous passing reference to a city along the coast of Turkey *which was destroyed, they say, for the sin of sodomy* (50), he leaves readers to wonder if he is referring indirectly to the accusation of homosexuality levelled against Alvaro de Luna by his enemies.

This, therefore, is the context, by no means intended to be completely described here, in which scholars of things Cypriot can begin to assess effectively Pero Tafur's account of his experiences with Cyprus. And these scholars should also be aware that Tafur is conscious of the tradition in which he is writing. In 1403, King Henry III of Castile sent an embassy to the Mongol lands of Emperor Tamburlaine, and, upon their return, the leaders of this expedition wrote a detailed account of their travels (published also in English translation in 1859). Tafur tells us in his narrative (165) that he discussed this expedition with one of the travellers. It would be surprising, also, if a man like Tafur, who displays knowledge of things Jewish, did not know of the famous Spanish rabbi Benjamin of Tudela who left an account of a journey he made around 1160 to many of the lands Tafur visited, including Cyprus. Rabbi Benjamin of Tudela's journey took place about fifty years after 1109 when Jews were attacked on a massive scale in Spain and when the anger against Jews and converts had not yet subsided even after fifty years; during those fifty years many Jews must have left Spain for the lands Rabbi Benjamin of Tudela visited. Likewise, Tafur's journey was made about forty-five years after the massacres of 1391.

Tafur is quite conscious, therefore, that his narrative fits into a long-standing tradition that links Spain with the struggle against the Moors, for Jerusalem, to find Prester John, to open up the spice routes to India. In this tradition, Jews always played an important role, with their ancient trading networks throughout the known world. In fact, in 1486, Columbus found himself in the famous Jewish community of Córdoba to exploit such networks. It is believed that Tafur may have died around 1484 (Ramírez 283), but if he were still alive, as alderman of Córdoba, Tafur certainly would have discussed his travels with Columbus in 1486.

II. TEXTS and CONTEXTS

Passage 1: Tafur tells about the Genoese at Famagusta and about the Mala Paga prison

Tafur first mentions Cyprus towards the end of the very first paragraph of his narrative after the prologue. The paragraph begins by describing Tafur's progress on his way to join Count Niebla in an attempt to take Gibraltar from the Moors. Tafur was not prepared to fight because he had already made preparations to leave on his journey, and he was ill. The attempt failed, and Count Niebla was killed. Tafur returned to the port of Barrameda and boarded a Genoese carrack at Cadiz. The ship stopped at a town called Arcilla on the African coast, at Ceuta, Malaga, Cartagena, and along the Mediterranean coast past the islands of Majorca and Menorca, past Barcelona, the Gulf of Lyons (where a storm almost destroyed the ship), past Nice, Savona, and on to Genoa. As he describes Genoa, Tafur mentions that it owns Famagusta in Cyprus. He also mentions that he visited the Mala Paga prison, a place where famous Cypriots were jailed; although Tafur does not relate the prison to Cyprus, his mention of it is included in this section because of its role in Cypriot history.

Paragraph 1, (fol. 5v, lines 4–10, fol. 5v, line 22 to fol. 6r, line 2; Jiménez 12–14): *This city [Genoa], for all its patrimony, has community rule, and because of its industry and expertise, it owns many cities and towns and castles on the mainland, and many islands in the sea; it owns Chios and Mytilene, and on the island of Cyprus, it owns a city they call Famagusta which they won when they captured the King of Cyprus and brought him there to Genoa, him and his wife. And the father of this [reigning] king [of Cyprus] was born there in the lighthouse tower; and his name was Janus because he was born in Genoa*[3] *(12–13)... This city, in the factions that they had, the Duke of Milan entered as lord with one faction, and while I was there,*[4] *they rebelled against the Duke and killed a captain he had there, whom they call Miçer Lopiçin de Alasar, and they destroyed the castle that was on the edge of the city. There they showed me the Mala Paga*[5] *where those knights who were captured with the kings of Aragon and Navarre were held prisoner (14).*

Passage 2: Tafur stops at Cyprus en route to Jerusalem

Tafur left Genoa and made his way to Venice via Pisa, Florence, Bologna, and Ferrara (paragraphs 2 to 4). In Venice, Tafur learned that the pilgrim boats did not leave for Jerusalem before the month of May, leaving three whole months before he could embark. Tafur wanted to spend this time travelling through the Christian lands, but his friends persuaded him to leave that trip for his return from Jerusalem and to travel through Italy instead. In Italy, Tafur toured Rome, Viterbo, Nernia, Ternia, Spoleto, Perugia, Assisi, and Ravenna before he returned to Venice with more than a month to spare until the pilgrim boats left on Ascension Day (paragraphs 5–7). From Venice, Tafur sailed to Rhodes via Parenzo, Zaira, Ragusa, Velona, Corfu, Coron, Modone, and Crete (paragraphs 7–8). From Rhodes, he sailed past Cyprus on to Jaffa.

Tafur did not expect to stop at Cyprus on his way to Jerusalem because, he tells us (50), the plague there discouraged travellers and sea captains from stopping on the island.[6]

Paragraph 9, (fol. 17v, lines 7–21; Jiménez 50–51): *We left this island [Rhodes] and sailed all that day and night, and morning found us at Castelrosso which belongs to Armenia and is an island and great fortress of the religious Order of Rhodes. From there we left taking the route to Cyprus along the coast of Turkey where the great lords of Turkey live, the great Caraman, and the lord of Candelor, and the lord of Satalia, and other great lords. There they showed us a city which was destroyed, they say, for the sin of sodomy. And we sailed a lot in three days, passing the Gulf of Satalia, and we went towards the island of Cyprus, along its outer part* [that is, along the coast of Cyprus that faces the Mediterranean sea rather than the coastline], *towards a city they call Paphos, uninhabited because of bad air and bad water. And because those who go to Jerusalem have the custom on the way there of not disembarking at the island, nothing more will be said here about Cyprus for that reason, and it will be discussed later in its place. From Paphos, making our way to Jaffa, which is the port for Jerusalem, we travelled for three days and as many nights, for there are three hundred and fifty miles from shore to shore* [between Paphos and Jaffa]. *The fourth day dawned on us on the beach of the Holy Land, and because in that part the land is flat, the entrance to Jaffa cannot be seen.*

From Jaffa, Tafur travelled the pilgrim route to Jerusalem, stopping at Rama to copy the inscriptions on the tombstones of Godfrey of Bouillon and his brother Baldwin, visiting Mount Zion, the Holy Sepulchre, Calvary, the Mount of Olives, Pilate's House, Bethlehem, Elijah's house, St. Anne's house, the house where Peter denied Jesus, Absalom's tomb, and making a daring visit in Moorish garb inside what he calls "the Temple of Solomon," the history and appearance of which he describes. When he inquired about visiting the monastery of St. Catherine on Mount Sinai, he was advised that he had just missed the caravan and should go to Cyprus to arrange for permission from the Sultan of Egypt.

Passage 3: Tafur returns to Cyprus for permission to visit Mount Sinai

Paragraph 9, (fol. 22r, lines 2–8; Jiménez 64–65): *During all these days, I had enquired about how I might go to Saint Catherine on Mount Sinai, which is close to the Red Sea. And I found out that the guides and the camels had left with an ambassador from Turkey who was going to the Sultan at Babylonia* [Old Cairo],[7] *and because of this my way was blocked. And I would have stayed there, if necessary, for another year. And the warden* [of the Holy Sepulchre] *advised me to go to Cyprus, and that there I would find the Cardinal, brother of the old king,*[8] *and that he would give me a way to get to Babylonia, and from there to Mount Sinai; and I did that* (64–65).

From Jerusalem, Tafur went to Rama, then to Jaffa where he embarked for Damascus, Tyre, Ascalon, Acre, and Beirut.

Passage 4: The King of Cyprus sends Tafur on a mission to the Sultan of Egypt

Paragraph 9, (fol. 22r, line 23 to fol. 28r, line 15; Jiménez 66–85): *We left Beirut along the coast of Syria up to Armenia, where they say Antioch was, and from there* [that is, the coast of Armenia] *they showed it* [Antioch] *to us. And going further along the coast, we saw the castle of Curco, which of old used to be called Colcos, where Medea was, and the island where the Golden Ram roamed. And this castle belongs to the kings of Cyprus, and because of that they are all called the kings of Armenia.*[9] *In this part of Armenia there is a high mountain range that they call Black Mountain, on which Noah's Ark is claimed to have come to rest after the flood. In front of this castle is the island and kingdom of Cyprus, and that part opposite Armenia is the city of Famagusta, an ancient city, which the Genoese won when they took the King of Cyprus captive and brought him to Genoa, him and his wife; and there the Queen gave birth to a son whose name was Janus, father of this king who now reigns. This place is deserted because of its bad air and bad water. They say that there is a lake there that they call Gostanza, and that that [lake] causes the ill health in the land, although all the realm of Cyprus is unhealthy for the most part. We arrived there at daybreak and we anchored to take on certain merchandise; and I said goodbye to the captain and to my friends, and I had all my belongings unloaded on shore and ordered that animals be fetched for myself and my retinue and for what had to be transported, and I left immediately, and took the road for Nicosia, which is ten leagues from there; this is the major city of the kingdom and the most healthy, where the kings usually are and all the lords of their land.*[10] *And because it was late, I stopped at a village two leagues from there, and upon arriving, I had such a terrible headache that I thought I was going to die; and from there that same pain went down to my chest and to my stomach and to my belly and to my hips and to my thighs and to my knees down to my feet; and it stayed all that night with me and the next day until vespers, so that I kept thinking that if each pain should have lasted three hours I would have died. And that afternoon I left there and went to the city of Nicosia where the king has his court, and I went to an inn where I spent that night. The next day, in the morning, as I was listening to mass in the church of Saint George, a squire of Lady Agnes, sister of King Janus, came up to me [saying] that she sent [him] to call me. And after mass was finished I went with the squire to the lady's palace and paid homage to her; and she received me very humanely, wishing to know who I was and where I came from and where I was going. And after a long conversation, she ordered that I be lodged in her house and that all the necessary things be given to me and my retinue. This lady was very noble, and she never married, as a young virgin, and she always was in the King's council, and by her vote the kingdom was ruled most of the time; she was probably fifty years of age.*[11] *And after I had rested that day, the next day the lady went to see the King, her nephew, and the Cardinal, her brother, and she took me with her;*

and there I paid homage to the King and to the Cardinal, his uncle, and they received me gladly. And there I told them how my journey had progressed: first of all that I had come there to visit the King and his court, and also to find a way to go to Babylonia and to Mount Sinai. And for all those reasons I had carried letters of recommendation from King John [II of Spain] *to the Cardinal of Cyprus who at that time was in Italy*[12] *and now I found him here; and he told me that I should be happy, that he would give me good provisions for what I wanted. And at that time, Mosen Suarez,*[13] *Admiral of Cyprus, was present, and he came up to me in a very homely way, showing himself to be a Castilian like me, and he earnestly requested of the King and the Cardinal and the lady, Madame Agnes, that they let me be his guest; and he insisted so much, especially with the lady, that he succeeded and then I went with him. He is a knight, native of Segovia, from the Cernadilla family, and as a young man travelling the world, he found himself in Cyprus on the day of the battle which the king fought against the Sultan's forces; and he placed his own person valiantly in such a way that he freed the king's life from danger and was taken prisoner with him and carried to Babylonia. And the Moors have a custom that no one should ride on horseback unless he were a Christian and a renegade; and on the day the king entered Babylonia captive, they brought two horses, one for the king and the other for Mosen Suarez; and when they were brought before the Sultan, he ordered, upon finding out the truth as it had taken place, that equal honor be paid to him* [Mosen Suarez] *as to the king. And after a few days, talking about ransom for the King, the Sultan said to Mosen Suarez that if he intended to achieve freedom for the king, that he would free him on his* [Mosen Suarez's] *oath, and that he should go and return with the ransom money, or at least with his person. Mosen Suarez promised this to him, and the Sultan ordered that everything he needed be given to him, and they even say that he asked him in what manner he wanted to come dressed, and he replied that* [he wanted to travel] *in Syrian fashion. And the Sultan ordered that it be done immediately, and he gave him leave, and he left and came to Cyprus; and there with the Cardinal and with Lady Agnes and others in the council they ordered that certain knights be sent to the Christian kings and princes so that they would help in the rescue of the king. (And I saw there in Cyprus the knight whom they call Jacobo Guiri who came here* [to Spain]*). And in like manner it fell to the lot of Mosen Suarez to go to the Pope. And after some time they all returned, each with what they brought and with what they were able to get from their* [allotted] *kingdom, and the ransom for the king was raised. And Mosen Suarez with others from the council of the king took that sum, which was three hundred thousand ducats, and went to bring their king. And when they reached Babylonia and the Sultan found out about it, he gave an order to go out to receive him, and he paid him as much respect as if he were his son. And there the order for the release of the king was given in this manner: the Sultan received that amount of gold, and in addition the King of Cyprus was obliged to give him one thousand ducats every year; and with this his case was closed. And the Sultan ordered that the necessary things and ships be readied to take him to his kingdom; and to Mosen Suarez he gave many favors; and to a leading interpreter of the Sultan, a native of Castile, a Jew from Seville who had apostatized in Babylonia, they send two hundred ducats every year for services rendered to the king during his imprisonment.*[14] *And the king, when he reached his kingdom and took counsel with his grandees, led Mosen Suarez by the hand and seated him at his side saying that if* *he had no legitimate son he would leave him the kingdom as an inheritance; and right away he sent for an illegitimate daughter of his who was there and he married her to him and made him his admiral, and he made her a [legal] heir to the kingdom.*[15] *After I had spent four or five days in the home of the admiral, Mosen Suarez, the Cardinal sent for me and told me that I should go and hear mass with the king, and that he would give me provisions for the journey to Babylonia, and that I would dine with him. And after mass was heard, the king went aside to one corner of the church with the Cardinal and with his aunt and some of his advisors; and the Cardinal told me on behalf of the king that he knew that I wanted to go to Babylonia and to Mount Sinai, and since the king had to send an ambassador to the Sultan on the king's business, that he was asking me to accept that [assignment], and that the king would be very much indebted to me for it. And I understood very well that the Cardinal had taken that stance because it was my duty, and I replied that I was very pleased to serve him because he was a king and a Christian and affiliated to the nation of France. The king directed me to dine there with him and with the Cardinal, and there he gave instructions for my journey. And from there I left for the port of Paphos where the king had given instructions, on account of the great plague [below] in Paphos, that I be lodged in a village on top of a mountain, which is a salutary place; and I stayed in the house of Diego Thenorio, a Castilian squire, and I had great pleasure in his company. And after three days an eighteen-bench skiff arrived in the port of Paphos which was to carry me, and it carried the King's interpreter who was to go with me, and many food supplies, as from a king's household, and the provisions for what I had to do with the Sultan. On the second day we set sail and travelled the sea for eleven days, sometimes with a good wind. Finally we arrived at the port of Damietta, where the river Nile, which has its source in the Earthly Paradise, enters the Mediterranean sea; and there we entered up the river, about a mile and a half, to the city of Damietta, which is about the size of Salamanca, with an abundance of bread and grapes and all kinds of fruit, and even more so of sugarcane fields,*[16] *a flat city without walls and without a castle, very hot, to an extreme degree, with very cool dwellings, with so many weasels in the streets and houses that there are more [weasels] than in those places where there are many mice. There I saw [for the] first [time] pigeons that carry the letter in a feather in their tail; this is done by carrying them from the place where they are raised to another place, and, putting the letter on it, they set it loose and it returns to its home. This is done in order to receive news fast about people who come by sea or by land, so that they not be taken unprepared, because they live without fortresses and without a wall. As soon as I arrived, I was taken to the Governor, and I told him that I was on my way to the Sultan, and that he should give me a skiff to go in, because mine was not for travelling on river water; and he gave directions that I be housed in his home while provision was being made. And while I was there, some Moors came saying that I was Catalan, that they had seen me eat with the lord of Candelor, and that they wanted to prove it. And they brought two Turks, pagan nobles, who were there, so that they could tell the truth. And they came to me and looked at me and said that the Moors were lying. And I asked, "If the Turks had said otherwise, what would have become of me?" And they said death, that whatever the Turks say is approved as truth. This place has more dates than any other place in the world. The River Nile that passes through it (which is one of two branches that diverge at about a day's journey away from Babylonia) rises suddenly in the month of September, when I was there, and fills up all the land; and with the high water many fish from the sea come along the riverbank up to the houses; and since most houses have doors facing the riverbank to fetch water because of the great heat, sometimes big fishes enter those doors and run aground on the floor, and there they kill them. There are on that riverbank some beasts which they call cockatrice that breed in the water, and which there is no man or beast that they can reach in the water that they do not kill; and they say that in the water they flee from the water-buffalo; and for this reason, since in all those parts there is no bridge nor can any be built because of the deep sands, and in order to pass from one bank to the other poor people would need to rent a boat, they mount those water-buffaloes and cross the river safely afloat without any danger whatever.*[17] *These beasts are used to coming out of the water five or six paces, and when the sun is out they are drowsy; and those who go to kill them carry a lance shaft with a barbed crossheaded harpoon on its tip which tightens as it strikes and binds in the flesh when tugged. And on the* [other] *end of it* [the shaft] *a cord one hundred and fifty fathoms long, or more, is tied; and as he goes up to it, if he can wound it under its side (because anywhere else would not work) the arrow enters; and the skin there is very soft, and as it feels it is wounded it heads for the water, and they give it rope until it gets tired, and then they pull it on land and carry it through the villages and towns, demanding* [rewards]*, as they do in Castile, the one who kills the wolf. This* [beast] *is in every way fashioned like a lizard; its teeth match male and female top and bottom, and for this reason they say that when they bite on anything they cannot let it go so easily. These* [beasts] *flee on land from anything, because land is strange to them. I saw many of them on this riverbank. Many people say (I myself did not see it) that on this same riverbank other beasts breed which are* [like] *horses, no more no less, except that they have a mouth as wide as the face, and they come out dripping with water to graze; and there they set some covered pits for them, like* [the ones] *they call in Castile wolf traps, and there they kill them; and these do no harm neither in the water nor out of it. This water on this riverbank is the best that I found; it well resembles water from Paradise. In the time that I was there I never drank but of this water, being able to drink good wine. Here in this place there are so many quails that, as is the custom in Castile, they sell ten for a maravedi; and they kill them with hounds, because they stun them* [motionless] *with a stick with two or three small bells on the end. Here I stayed eight days; then the Governor made me get a ship they call "gerba"* [djibba or felucca] *to go to Babylonia, which are as long as a great galley and all made with cabins for lodging from one end to the other, and flat-bottomed so that they can sail in shallow water. They carry heavy cargoes and hoist the sail as high as a carrack, except that it is narrow and lateen as a galley's; and it often happens, in the season of the rising of the river, that they travel by sail and oars and not move a step ahead unless they find some calm water or cause people to disembark on land so that they can tow it with long ropes. They carry three drums continuously, one at the poop, another at the prow, and another at midship, to scare away the cockatrices I spoke about. No one dares to take water from the river by hand, but they tie the vessel by the handle and draw water that way. After I left Damietta, continuing my journey up along the riverbank, I found it on one bank and the other all populated with villages next to the water, and I went to that spot where the branches divide, this one to where I was going, and the other* [branch] *that goes close to*

Alexandria. There is a tribe of people in Babylonia who shave their heads and chins and eyebrows and eyelids and seem to live like mad people, saying that that is saintliness and that to serve God they despise the world and its pomp, which is what they shaved away. And some of them go about loaded with horns, others smothered in honey and feathered, and others with lances and burning lanterns hanging from them, and others with bows with the arrow ready [to shoot] on the bowstring, and like this in diverse ways, saying that they are going in pursuit of Christians; and the Moors treat them with great reverence. And one day I found a fleet of them, and I asked where they were going, and they told me to throw themselves in a fire with the Christian dogs to see who would burn. On this island of Alexandria I talked about they make much flax from which such fine canvas sails are made. And from there, continuing our journey, in seven days we went into Babylonia, and we disembarked at the port where there is a public granary where all the Christians dock, and we unloaded all our belongings from the ship and that night we stayed in that house. The morning of the next day I ordered that well equipped donkeys be rented with their saddles and bridles, very fast walkers, and a man to guide us to the house of the chief interpreter of the sultan; and we had to walk from daybreak to midday to his house. And as we reached him, I gave him the letters and greetings from the King of Cyprus and, in addition, two hundred ducats that the king sent him which his father had left instructions for him to do in this way for all his life, because of the service he did him in prison; the chief interpreter received us very well and lodged [us] inside his home. And I was there two days before I saw the sultan; and in those two days, while the interpreter was discussing many things with me and asking me where I was from, he came to learn from me that I was Castilian, a native of Seville; and he was very pleased with me because he too was from Seville, and as a child he was carried to Jerusalem with his father who was Jewish; and his father died, and he became a Moor; and first they called him Haym, and now Saym. He was keen to find out about me, who I was and how I came; and I did not hide any of my business from him, so that I could make good use of him and his advice; and, in this [same] way, he did it [to me]. I was so well treated by him in his house, letting me go among his wives and children, as if I were his own son, and he kept telling me that this was the greatest honor that he could grant me, and that it seemed likely that I was from his nation because his children loved me so much. This was probably a man of about ninety years, but in spite of that, he did not stop engendering, because even while I was there one of his wives gave birth to a son. He had four Christian wives, like those who are bought on the Black Sea,[18] in as much as they would consider it a great dishonor to marry a native Moor. Those three days I spent with him without seeing the Sultan, he showed me so many things that it would take long to write them. On the third day he took the letters I was bringing to the Sultan, and he took them and showed them to him, and they took counsel as to the reply; and that night he brought me the same letters sealed, and told me that because I was his countryman, he wanted to let me know that the Sultan had already seen those letters, and that they considered it a discredit not to respond immediately, and that for that reason they are accustomed to see [the letters] first; and that I should propose my business not letting on that I had been apprised of that [practice]. The morning of the next day, he ordered that animals be readied for me and my retinue, and as the sun rose, we went to the Sultan's house. And before we got there, we went along the streets eating and drinking, because men walk about carrying cookery with ready-made food, others selling fruit, others selling water, and others other things. We reached the Great Mosque, which is a good thing to see, but I have seen many better in Christian lands; then we came to a large square where there were many people on horseback and some pitched tents, as they call them, and outside the city, likewise, very many people on horseback, because that was the day that the Sultan was given a military salute; and if I do not speak about the number of people on horseback as well as on foot, I do so in order not to say something that would be hard to believe, although anything can be said and believed in these parts, no doubt. And we arrived at the gate of the Sultan's quarters, and there we left the animals and climbed the steps to the door; these quarters are probably as big as Villareal. And walking the streets, I saw many people on one side and the other, and they told me that those were the mamelukes, whom here [in Spain] *we call apostate renegades, a large crowd of people; and these are the ones the Sultan orders bought with his money around the Black Sea and in all the provinces where Christians are sold. And when they bring them there they make them Moors and teach them the religion and how to ride and use the bow; and once they are examined by the Chief Doctor* [of religious law], *they are paid their wages and their rations and are sent to the city; one cannot be sultan or admiral or receive any honor or position whatever unless one belongs to these renegades, nor can any Moor by birth ride on horseback without dying for it. These are the ones who have all the honor of chivalry, and their sons a little less, and their grandsons less, and from then on they remain Moors by birth; all this to augment their religion, and for this they call him* [the Sultan] *the increaser of the law of Mohammed.*[19] *Women do not have this prerogative, but a Moor would sooner take a Christian woman* [as a wife] *without dowry than a Moorish woman however well endowed, especially if he is a Moor by birth. Still walking through those streets, we came to a gate that was closed, and they opened for us and we went in and found a big plaza full of knights placed by rank up against the walls; and from there they opened another gate for us and we found a square of knights in that very same ranking order. Then they opened another gate for us, and we found another square in the very same ranking order, except that it was of black men with clubs in their hands; and there the interpreter made me stay with my retinue until he returned to me; and after a short while he returned to me and took me through a gate to a great plaza where there were many knights in the order I spoke about; and in the middle of the plaza there was a large and luxurious tent with its reviewing platforms where the Sultan was to dine and the military salute was to be made to him. And near there, a pavilion portal was set up where a high platform was placed and a throne, where the Sultan was to dismount. And the Chief Interpreter told me that I should wait in the middle of that plaza, and that the Sultan would come out and pass close to me; and that I should not make him any curtsy whatever because that* [is what] *they are used to do as an insult to Christians. And while* [waiting] *there, they opened a large gate and the Sultan rode out, and ahead of him, his son on foot with about two hundred knights, and he passed like that close to me and went to sit on the throne I mentioned. A few days before, the Sultan had ordered freed from prison a son of the Treasurer of the Sultan he had succeeded, who had owned a great quantity of wealth in gold as well as in pearls and precious stones and other things of value, and to whom at that event, in order to please him and restore him to his grace, he sent a reddish-black horse shod in gold with the bridle and saddle also adorned in the same gold, in the front saddle-bow a spinel ruby which they say weighed a "rótulo" [an Egyptian pound][20] and a half, which seemed as large as a medium-sized orange; in the back saddle-bow, three spinel rubies as large as hen's eggs, and a scimitar which was worth a large sum of gold; and its covering was of white damask bordered with a hem of rich pearls. The Chief Interpreter came for me and told me that I should make a show of kissing the ground before approaching him, and he took the letters which I had and he put them on my head and on my mouth as a greeting and gave them to the Sultan; and since the letters were in another language, he read them in Turkish, because before the Sultan and in his court no other language is spoken. They say that this came about when the Turk adopted the religion of Mohammed, which is a short time ago, and that this ceremony is done to honor him. The Sultan asked me about the King of Cyprus and about the Cardinal, his uncle, and about Mosen Suarez, and about some people in the kingdom, and as soon as I had answered him, he told me right away that he was pleased to do what I had come about. This was: that the King was sending to request that [the Sultan] not send him those mamelukes he usually sends every year for the tribute, because they cause him very great expense, and that he [the King] would send it four months thence; the other [request was] that he [the Sultan] should accept it [the tribute] in camlets at the price they are worth in Babylonia; the other [request was] that he let him [the King] sell his salt, which is a great [source of] income, in all of Syria without paying taxes; and all of this was granted. The Sultan then ordered that they house me well and that they give me all things necessary; and so it was done. On this day, the Sultan gave me an item of clothing that he usually gives as a mark of lordship to the King of Cyprus; and it was of a rich Oriental green and red fabric worked in gold and lined with patterns of ermine. Then the Sultan came down from that throne to the tent, and they gave him the military salute there, and fed him; and there I took leave of him for this day. And while I was there, about one hundred men came in bringing a Moor on their shoulders, and they put him on the ground, and he was promptly stripped naked and given two hundred lashes with rods on his stomach and back; and they say that all the criminal justice is done before the Sultan. And we returned through the same place, and we did not find any of those whom we had seen on the way there, except the blacks; and once we got down to the great plaza, we rode on our animals, and we did not find in that plaza or in the tents any knights, only poor men with sieves sifting the sands; and I asked what was that, and he replied to me that they were men of fortune who look for anything that may have fallen on the ground from such a large crowd of people as was gathered there. This day we had to travel until sunset to get back to the [Chief Interpreter's] house. The next day we rested, and I ordered that the Sultan's dispatch be sent to the King of Cyprus in that skiff of his that remained in Damietta, and that the skiff should come for me two months from then, inasmuch as I intended to go to Saint Catherine on Mount Sinai. And after I sent the dispatch to the King of Cyprus, I stayed in Babylonia close to one month, looking at many things, and most strange, especially [in comparison] to those of our nation; and certainly I was most fortunate in having such guidance as that of the Chief Interpreter, for he took great pleasure in working with me in what I wanted.*

Passage 5: Tafur mentions Cyprus to Niccolo Conti

During the weeks (almost a month) Tafur says he spent in Babylonia after he sent the Sultan's reply to the King of Cyprus, Tafur visited the garden at Matarea, famous for its balsam, the granaries of Joseph, a zoo with elephants (87), and a giraffe (88); and then he returned to the city he calls Babylonia. He asked the Sultan's permission to leave Cairo for Mount Sinai, and the Sultan granted his request and outfitted him well for the fifteen-day trip across the desert. Tafur described how monasteries came to be built in honor of Saint Catherine on the top and at the bottom of Mount Sinai; how the saint's body came to be moved from the monastery on top (where Moses received the law and saw the burning bush) to the one on the bottom; how difficult it is to see the saint's body; how the monks live and receive their income; and how the Patriarch at Alexandria elects the patriarch that is sent to Prester John in India. After three days at the monastery of Saint Catherine, Tafur inquired "secretly" of the Prior how he could pass over into India. The Prior told him that the huge caravan from India was due in two or three days; it came after four or five days, and Tafur went to meet it. In that caravan was the famous Niccolo Conti with whom Tafur spoke at great length. This portion of their conversation below is selected because it mentions Cyprus: as part of his strategy of identifying himself as much as possible with the person to whom he is speaking, Tafur first introduced himself to Conti as an Italian who had grown up in Cyprus.

Paragraph 9, (fol. 31r, line 14 to fol. 31v, line 5; Jiménez 95–96): *I went along the coast of the Red Sea, which is half a league from Mount Sinai, to see how the caravan [from India] came, and I found that a Venetian was coming there whom they called Nicolo de Conto [sic], a gentleman by birth; and he brought with him his wife and two sons and a daughter, whom he had in India; and they came, he and they, as converted Moors, because they had forced them to apostatize in Mecca, which is their holy place. And he, as soon as he saw me, came up to me and asked me who I was and what I was doing there, and what was my trade; and I told him that I was from Italy and had grown up with the king of Cyprus, and that I had come to Babylonia on his bidding, to the Sultan, and that with his permission I had come there and even intended to go on to India. And he replied immediately that I should not do it, and that even if I wanted to do it, that I would not be able to accomplish it. And I, still insisting on going there, he spoke to me and implored me to tell him who I was, and that he would do me a great service, that was, that he would tell me the way I would have to do it, and that I could well trust him because he was a Christian as I was, and that he would tell me the story of his life and how he had come there. And I, seeing that he was a serious person and discreet and of good bearing, told him that I was a gentleman and knight, native of Spain, and how I came to the Holy Sepulchre and from there to Babylonia with the intent of coming to Mount Sinai and from there going on to India.*[21]

After listening to Conti's story, Tafur decided to change his mind about going to India. Instead, he left Mount Sinai in the company of Niccolo Conti, questioning him for fifteen days (until they got back to Babylonia) about India and Prester John (96–111). At Babylonia, Tafur and Conti agreed to meet each other every day at Saint Martha's church, where Pedro de la Randa is buried. The choice of church is not accidental, and Tafur relates the story of Pedro de la Randa (who died instead of renouncing his religion) as that story was told to him by the Sultan's chief interpreter who witnessed it all (111–116). From Babylonia, Tafur returns to Alexandria and then back to Damietta to await the ship that would take him back to Cyprus.

Passage 6: Tafur returns the Sultan's reply to Cyprus

Paragraphs 11–13, (fol. 38v, line 18 to fol. 41r, line 9; Jiménez 119–126): *And when I had seen it* [the city of Alexandria] *well, I set out on land and went to Damietta, and I did not find the skiff which the King of Cyprus had given me; and I waited for it for eight days, and it came, for it had gone towards the coast of Jerusalem. And there* [at Damietta], *I received much honor*[able treatment] *from the Governor, because I brought him letters of recommendation on my behalf from the Sultan's Chief Interpreter; and he* [the Chief Interpreter] *sent to ask him if he had some cockatrice skin that he might send to the King of Cyprus who had asked him for it. And he offered one that they had killed and it was fresh and smelled very bad, so much so that it would have been better to have brought a very beautiful daughter of the Governor whom he had there than the cockatrice skin. And I set out to sea and in seven days landed at the port of Paphos, where I had embarked, a very afflicted place; and on the very day that I arrived, the Bishop and two of his squires had died;*[22] *and God was merciful to me in that as soon as I put my foot on the ground, right away I rode on the animals of the Bishop and his men and left for the court of the King of Cyprus which was in Nicosia. And my interpreter whom the King had given to me went ahead to tell the king and the cardinal, and they sent instructions that I should stop that night in a village, because they wanted to receive me honorably on the morning of the next day; and so they did. The morning of the next day, I found many of those lords of the king's court who came out to receive me, and they accompanied me to the King in person; and when I arrived I found the King and the Cardinal and many of the nobles with them, and I was very well received and treated with such humaneness, as if I were a native of their country, and* [they were] *thanking God that I had returned to safety from such a long voyage, and thanking me over and over again on behalf of the King for what I had done in his service, and offering me whatever I might like. And after this, I took leave of the King; and the Admiral who was there took me to his house, as usual, where I was very well hosted. The morning of the next day, there was a great murmuring among all the people, and everyone armed themselves, especially the Cardinal and Lady Agnes, his sister, against the king,* [wanting] *to kill or arrest a favorite that he* [the King] *had, whom they called Jacobo Guiri* [James Gurri],[23] *a judge by profession. The King fled to a fortress which they call the Citadel, which is at the end of the city, and there they laid siege around him and held such resolve with him that he should set this favorite aside from him, and that he* [the favorite] *should not enter his court for a year; and so the King swore to it and it was immediately accomplished, and they lifted* [their siege] *from over him. The next day following, the King sent for me, and before the Cardinal and some nobles he spoke to me and implored me to take from him whatever I pleased for the cost of my journey; and I replied that I was very grateful to him for that, [but] that I had enough for my return trip, and that I was requesting of him that he give directions to give me permission and a skiff that would take me to Rhodes; and I worked as hard as I could to leave and he to detain me; and he strongly requested that I should stay there eight days at least, and I, since I saw that he took pleasure in it, did it; and without doubt, in those days I could not have been better refreshed, and the ship was outfitted that was to take me; and I said goodbye to the King (and he certainly gave me leave against his will), and there he gave me his coat of arms, which I have today, and he gave me ten pieces of camlet and fine linen, and a leopard,[24] and as much provisions to get to Rhodes as would have lasted for a year. And at this time that I was there, two embassies came to the King of Cyprus (one from the Duke of Savoy, and another from a Duke of Germany) to arrange marriage, each of them, for his daughter; and I did not leave the matter settled with either of them, because it was being said that the Master of Rhodes was very eagerly bringing him another marriage [proposal] to a daughter of the Count of Urgel, sister of the wife of the Prince Don Pedro, regent of Portugal; but it seemed to me that what those in the King's council were stressing most was with the daughter of the Duke of Savoy, and I think that this was settled upon.[25] The King was a young man of about sixteen or seventeen years, and large in physique, although his legs were, without any doubt, as fat at the calves as at his thighs; a gracious man he was, and, for his age, with a rather good mind, and happy and well-disposed in body, especially in riding;[26] and, no doubt, if the land had not been so unsalutary, I would have been quite willing to serve him for a while, but it would have been almost impossible for a foreigner to be able to live in a land so afflicted, and for that reason, and because of the desire I had to return to Castile on account of the war against the Moors, I had to continue my journey as quickly as I could.*

[Paragraph 12] *I left the city of Nicosia and went to Aherines [Kyrenia] where the boat that was to take me to Rhodes was awaiting me; and this is an ancient city that Achilles built and from that fact it took the name; a small city but strong and well walled, and [a] good port though small, but chained and well guarded; here the present King escaped, and the Cardinal, his uncle, and Lady Agnes and many others of the kingdom, when King Janus was captured.[27] This is the healthiest land there is in all of Cyprus, because it is exposed to the west wind. And there I found a merchant ship that the king had ordered be prepared for me, to take me to Rhodes, and another merchant ship which carried merchandise in company with it. And we left the port and went to the point of the cape of Saint Pifani and we were there until noon; and we hoisted sail and set out to sea along the gulf of Satalia, the route to Turkey; and in less than two hours we saw a galley of Turks coming, and it was coming against us to take us and break us into pieces, because of a skiff which the Catalans had taken from Turks in the harbor of Cyprus; and we, full sail and oars, and they likewise, in such a way that no prayers were lacking there, with hands well worked at rowing. A boatswain of a Catalan galley, who had killed a nephew of the captain, was travelling with me; and he* [the captain] *had ordered him to be hanged from the lateen yard, and the rope broke on him, and I pleaded so much that he should give him to me since God had done so much for him; and he was persuaded; and because of this we escaped, because he knew a great deal about sailing; he lightened the load our merchant ship was carrying so that it could sail faster; and the other with merchandise refused to toss it into the sea; and when it was late and the sun was about to set, the Turks caught up with it and sank them all, and in the confusion they made with them, we had time to distance ourselves a little; and when night fell, we hung the sail as far as we could, and we all took hands to the oars and worked for half an hour* [turns] *as hard as we possibly could; and since it was a dark night, we lowered the sail and took to the right, rowing very quietly so that the oars made no sound, and the galley passed very close to us and did not see us. The Catalan boatswain said that it was necessary to make another better manoeuver, that the galley would head for land and wait, since ours was a small ship, and that they would have us in their hands; and we headed for the sea, and, as for the galley, we saw it go towards the land; and at midnight a meridional*[28] *wind rose up with force on the sea, and every wave thrust us from side to side. How much more would I have preferred to have fallen into the hands of the Turks than to be drowned in such a place! There they wanted to throw one of my men overboard, except that we defended him very well. With this storm* [also, luck] *we rushed towards Castelrosso and arrived there at the* [canonical] *hour of terce* [nine o'clock in the morning]*, and the galley had left there less than two hours before. We disembarked on land, because it is a good harbor, and we climbed up, because it is a great fortress, and there we rested, as one who escapes from a great plague. This castle belongs to the Religious Order of Rhodes, is part of the province of Armenia, even though it is an island, and it is so rocky that no beast can climb to the top; and below, at the entrance to the harbor, it has some salt-ponds, belonging to the Knights of Rhodes, which are of great revenue.*

[Paragraph 13] *We left the island of Castelrosso setting the course for Rhodes with great fear of that galley; and we had bad weather at sea but in two days journey we arrived at Rhodes and entered the harbor; and straightway I went to stay with Friar Nuño de Cabrera, a good knight, a countryman of ours from Castile and* [a member] *of the Order, and also among those there who had most wealth and about whom most mention is made; and he received me most happily and lovingly; and I was treated by him so humanely that, had it not been for the good company he kept with me (for I could not have been better nor more mercifully served in my own house), I would have kept thinking of dying after the hardship I had passed through. On the second day after my arrival, I had to go to the Grand Master of Rhodes to give him certain letters from the King of Cyprus which he had entrusted to me about their affairs;*[29] *and Friar Nuño de Cabrera and other Castilian knights accompanied me, and also* [knights] *from other nations, especially French* [knights]*, because they mingle a great deal with* [knights] *of our nation; and when I reached the Grand Master, I found him gravely ill with a pain in his side, but he immediately dispatched the reply to the King of Cyprus; and I left him and went back to the house, and that night he died of that illness.*[30]

Tafur then devotes an entire paragraph (#14) to the system for electing a new Grand Master at Rhodes. From Rhodes, Tafur made his way to Constantinople with stops at Chios, Troy (which he fails to locate), Mytilene, Tenedos, Gallipoli, and Pera (paragraphs 15, 16). At the end of paragraph 16, Tafur states the main purpose of his travels, namely, to verify and re-establish his family's ancient link to the Emperors of Constantinople. Paragraphs 17 and 18 are devoted almost entirely to a conversation between Tafur and the Emperor of Constantinople concerning issues related to Tafur's lineage. Tafur sees the Emperor leave for a meeting with the Pope which took place on November 24, 1437; and, in the Emperor's absence, Tafur asked the Emperor's brother for leave to go to Adrianopolis where he observed Turkish customs (end of paragraph 18). Upon his return to Constantinople from Adrianopolis, Tafur spent eight days touring before he leaves for Trebizond and Kaffa. At Kaffa he contemplated visiting the kingdom of the Great Khan but is dissuaded. At the end of paragraph 19, Tafur explicitly compares Christians living under the Grand Khan with *mudéjares*, Moslems living under Christian kings in Spain; this comparison makes it almost certain that Tafur also intended for readers to compare forced conversion in Egypt and in Spain.

Passage 7: Tafur mentions how Cypriots live in Venice

From Kaffa, Tafur made his way back to Venice by way of Trebizond, Constantinople, Pera, and from Pera by sea to Tenedos, Mitylene, Thessalonica, Modone, Corfu, Albania, Velona, Dalmatia, Ancona, Spoleto, Parenzo, and Venice. At this point approximately two-thirds through the text (paragraph 25), Venice becomes the base of operation for a visit to the Christian lands of Europe; and it is in this description of Venice that Tafur makes his last mention of Cyprus, as follows.

Paragraph 25, (fol. 65r, lines 3-12; Jiménez 209-10): *The houses of this city [Venice] are very striking and very tall and very closely stacked together, and with many chimneys, and they boast rich façades and windows onto the streets, richly worked in gold and blue, well marbled. And there are lords around, and even far from there, who boast of having a home in the city because it is so much worth it to have its benefit whenever they might need it,* [lords] *like the King of Cyprus, the Marquis of Ferrara, the Marquis of Mantua, the Marquis of Monferrat; and many other lords and knights have very magnificent homes there. I saw the Cardinal of Cyprus, brother of the king, who was staying there in his brother's house and who wanted to leave for Cyprus, and the galley that was to take him was tied up to the door of his house; and from there it received him and left with him through the middle of the city; and like this other big and mid-size ships are tied up to the doors of their lords.*

From Venice, Tafur travelled extensively to Ferrara, Milan, Basle, along the Rhine to Strassburg, Mainz, Koblenz, Cologne, Cleves, Niemegen, Bois le Duc, Brabant, Lille, Brussels, Bruge, Sluys, Ghent, Antwerp, Louvain and, retracing his steps, back to Basle. From Basle, he went East to Schaffhausen, Constance, Ulm, Nuremberg, Poland, Vienna, Budapest, Neustadt, Treviso, Padua, Florence, Pisa, Bologna, Ferrara, Venice, Ravenna, Ancona, Brindisi, by sea to Sicily, Messina, Palermo, Syracuse, Sardinia, and Tunis where the manuscript ends abruptly without describing the trip back to Spain.

III. APPENDICES

I append Professor Larkin's paleographic transcription of the original text for the convenience of those who would like to check on and improve my translation. I also append for convenience Book II, chapter 39 of Enguerrand de Monstrelet's *Chroniques*, together with the translation by Thomas Johnes, because it provides an important contemporary comparison with Tafur's version of the capture of King Janus.

Appendix 1

James B. Larkin, ed. *Pero Tafur: Andanças e viajes.* A line-numbered transcription of passages dealing with Cyprus in Ms.-1985 of the Library of the University of Salamanca.

[fol. 5v]

4 ellos el santo vaso que es de una esmeralda maravillosa reliquia. Esta cibdat co<n>

5 todo (13) su patrimonio se rige a comunidat, e por su industria e saber en la tierra firme

6 tiene muchas cibdades e villas e castillos, e en la mar muchas yslas tiene a

7 Cyjo, e a Metellin, en la ysla de Chipre tiene una cibdat que llama<n> famagosta

8 que ellos ganaro<n> quando prendieron al rey de Chipre, e lo truxero<n> alli a Genova

9 a el, e a su muger; e su padre deste Rey alli nasçio en la torre del faron, e ovo nom-

10 bre Ianus porque nasçio en Genova. Estos tiene<n> junto co<n> Costantinopla una

22 man a gran peoria suya. Esta çibdat en los vandos que ovieron con la una parte

23 entro el duque de Milan por señor, e estando yo alli se rebelaro<n> co<n>tra el Du<que>

24 e le mataron un capitan suyo que tenie alli que llaman miçero Lopiçin de

25 Alasar, e derribaron el castillo que estava en canto de la cibdat. Alli me mos-

[fol. 6r]

1 traro<n> la mala paga do estava<n> presos aquellos cavalleros que fuero<n> presos

2 con los Reyes de Arago<n> e de Navarra En este mar de Genova no<n> se cria pescado,

[fol. 17v] {7}

7 Partimos desta ysla e navegamos todo aquel dia e la noche, e amanesçimos sobre

8 Castilrojo, que es de Armenia ysla muy grande fortaleza de la Religion de

9 Rodas, de alli partimos façiendo la via de Chipre costeando por la Turquia

10 donde biven los mas grandes señores de la Turquia, el gran Caraman, e el se-

11 ñor de Candelor, e el señor de Satalias, e otros grandes señores. Alli nos mostra-

12 ron una cibdat que fue suvertida, dizen por el pecado de Sodomia. E nave-

13 gamos tanto en tres dias, pasando el golfo de Satalias e fuemos sobre la ysla de

14 Chypre por la parte de fuera, sobre una cibdat que llama<n> Bafa desabitada por

15 el mal ayre, e mal agua, e porque los que va<n> a Ierusalem an por uso a la yda

16 non desçender a la ysla por tanto aqui no se co<n>tara mas de Chipre que despues

17 en su lugar se (51) dira. De Bafa, façiendo n<uest>ro camino a Jafa que es el puerto de

18 Ierusalem que ay de tierra a tierra treçientas, e cinq<uen>ta millas, andovimos tres

19 dias con sus noches al quarto dia nos amanesçio sobre el esplaja de la tierra

20 santa, e porque en aquella parte la tierra es llana no<n> se puede conosçer la en-

21 trada de Jafa E quando el navio [. . . .]

[fol. 22r] {2}

2 [. . . . .] En todos estos dias yo avia buscado como pudiera yr

3 a santa Catalina de monte Synay, que es cerca del mar vermejo, e falle que los

4 trujamanes e los camellos eran partidos con un embaxador del Turco que yva

5 a Babylonia al Soldan, e por esto fue empachado mi camino, e yo quisiera estar alli

6 si menester fuera fasta otro año. E el guardian me co<n>sejo, que (65) yo viniese a Chi-

7 pre, e que alli fallaria al Cardenal hermano del Rey viejo, e que el me daria el ca-

8 mino como pasase en Babylonia, e de ay al mo<n>te de Synay, e yo fiçelo.

[fol. 22r] {23}

23 Partimos de Barut por la costa de Suria fasta la Armenia donde dizen

24 que fue Antiocha, e de alli nos la mostraron e yendo por la costa adela<n>te

25 vimos el castillo del Curco, que antiguame<n>te se llamava Colcos, donde

[fol. 22v]

1 fue Medea, e la ysla donde andava el carnero dorado e este castillo es de los

2 reyes de Chipre, e por eso todos se llama<n> reyes de Armenia. En esta

3 parte de Armenia esta una alta sierra que llama<n> montaña negra en la qual

4 se affirma aver quedado el arca de Noe despues del Diluvio. Enfrente deste cas-

5 tillo esta ysla e Reyno de Chipre E aquella parte de contra la Armenia

6 esta la cibdat de Famagosta antigua cibdat la qual los ginoveses ganaron

7 quando prendieron al Rey de Chypre, e lo truxero<n> a Genova a el e al su muger, e a-

8 lli pario la Reyna un fijo que ovo nombre Ianus padre deste Rey que agora es.

9 Este lugar es depoblado por mal ayre e mal agua. Dizen que esta alli un

10 lago que llaman la Gonstança, que el façe la poca salud en la tierra, aunque

11 todo el Reyno de Chypre por la mayor parte es mal sano. Alli llegamos al al-

12 va del dia, e surgimos por (67) tomar çiertas mercadurias, e yo despedime del Patron

13 e de mis amigos, e fiçe sacar todo lo mio en tierra, e fiçe buscar bestias para mi

14 e para los mios e para lo que avia de levar, e partime luego, e fuy el camino de

15 Nicosia, que es diez leguas de alli, esta es la mayor cibdat del Reyno e la mas

16 sana donde los Reyes siempre acostumbra<n> estar, e todos los señores de su Reyno.

17 E porque era tarde, yo me uve de detener en un aldea dos leguas de ay, e en alle-

18 gandome me dio tan grant dolor de cabeza que pense morir, e de alli aquel mesmo

19 dolor se me abaxo a los pechos, e al estomago, e a la barriga, e a las caderas, y

20 a los muslos, e a las rodillas fasta los pies, e turome toda esa noche, e otro dia

21 fasta viespras que pe<n>sava si cada uno me turara tres oras muriera, e aquella

22 tarde parti de ay, e fuy a la cibdat de Nicosia do el Rey tiene su corte, e fuy-

23 me a un meson do estuve aquella noche. Otro dia de mañana oyendo misa en una y-

24 glesia de Sant Jorje llego a mi un escudero de Madama Ynes hermana del Rey

25 Janus, que me embiava llamar E acabada la missa yo fuy co<n> el escudero al pala-

[fol. 23r]

1 çio de la Señora, e alli le fize revere<n>çia, e ella me resçibio muy humanamente

2 quiriendo saber de mi quien yo era, (68) e donde venia, e a do yva, e despues de

3 muchas fablas mandome aposentar dentro de su casa, e dar todas las cosas nes-

4 çesarias a mi e a los mios. Esta señora era muy noble, e nu<n>ca caso seyendo moça

5 virgen, e siempre estava en el consejo del Rey, e por su voto se regio las mas

6 veçes el Reyno serie de hedat de çinque<n>ta años. E despues que reposado ove

7 aquel dia, otro dia la señora fue a ver al Rey su sobrino, e al Cardenal su hermano

8 e me levo co<n>sigo, e alli fiçe revere<n>cia al Rey, e al Cardenal su tio, los quales me res-

9 çibieron alegreme<n>te, e alli les co<n>te el proçeso de mi camino prinçipalme<n>te yo era ve-

10 nido alli por visitar al Rey e su corte, lo otro para aver camino para pasar

11 a Babylonia, e al monte de Synay, e por quanto yo avia levado letras del Rey

12 Don Juan de recomendaçion, para el Cardenal de Chipre, el qual a la ora

13 estava en Ytalia, e entonçe lo falle alla. Dixome que oviese plaçer, que

14 el me daria bien aviamiento a lo que deseava. E aquella ora mosen Suarez

15 Almiralle de Chipre estava presente, e se llego a mi muy domesticame<n>te mos-

16 trandose ser castellano como yo, y suplico al Rey, e al Cardenal, e a la señora

17 Madama Ynes, que me dexasen yr por su huesped, e tanto lo porfio, e mas

18 co<n> la señora, (69) que lo acabo, y luego me fuy co<n> el. Este es un cavallero natural

19 de Segovia de los de Çernadilla, e seyendo moço, andando por el mu<n>do fallose

20 en Chypre el dia de la batalla, que el Rey peleo co<n> la ge<n>te del Soldan, e

21 asi fiço el valiente de la persona que escapo al Rey la vida, y fue preso co<n> el

22 e levado a Babylonia, e los moros acostumbra<n> que ninguno no<n> cavalgue en

23 cavallo si no fuere xpiano, e renegado, e este dia que entro en Babylonia el

24 Rey preso truxero<n> dos cavallos uno para el Rey, e otro para mosen Suarez

25 e quando fuero<n> levados ante el Soldan mando sabida la verdat como se avie

[fol. 23v]

1 avido, que ygual onrra como al Rey le fuese fecha. E a cabo de çiertos dias fabla<n>-

2 dose en el rescate del Rey, el Soldan dixo a mosen Suarez, que si el entendia a-

3 provechar en la deliberaçion del Rey, que el lo soltaria sobre su verdat, e que vini-

4 ese, e bolviese con recabdo, o a lo menos su persona. Mosen Suarez ge lo prometio

5 e el Solda<n> le mando dar todas las cosas que avia menester, e aun diçen que le pre-

6 gunto de que guisa queria venir Vestido, e respondio que al modo de la Suria

7 El Soldan lo mando cumplir luego, e lo licençio, e se partio, e vino a Chipre,

8 e alli con el Cardenal, e co<n> madama Ynes, (70) e los otros del co<n>sejo ordenaro<n> de

9 embiar çiertos cavalleros a los Reyes, e Prinçipes xpianos para que socorrie-

10 sen al rescate del Rey, e de alli vi yo en Chipre el cavallero que vino aca que

11 se llamava Jacobo Guiri, e asi mesmo mosen Suarez le cupo en suerte de

12 yr al Papa, en çierto tiempo todos fuero<n> de buelta, cada uno co<n> lo que trayen

13 e co<n> lo que pudiero<n> aver de su Reyno, e acabose la fiança del Rey, e Mosen

14 Suarez con otros del consejo del Rey levaro<n> aquella suma de oro, que fue tre-

15 çient(o/a?)s mil ducados, e fuero<n> a traer a su Rey. E quando llegaro<n> a Babylonia, e

16 el Soldan lo supo lo mando salir a resçebir, e le fizo ta<n>ta onrra como si fuera su

17 fijo, e alli se dio la orde<n> de la deliberaçion del Rey en esta guisa El Soldan res-

18 çibio aquella suma de oro, e mas el Rey de Chypre se le obligo de le dar cada año

19 ocho mil ducados, e co<n> esto se acabo su fecho. E el Soldan le ma<n>do aderesçar
20 las cosas nesçesarias, e navios que lo levasen a su reyno, e a Mosen Suarez
21 fiço muchas m<e>r<ce>d<e>s, e a un Trujaman mayor del Soldan natural de Castilla judio
22 de Sevilla, que se renego en Babilonia por serviçios que fiço al Rey en su prision
23 en cada año le lieva<n> doçientos ducados. E el Rey qua<n>do llego a su (71) Reyno, e tu-
24 vo consejo co<n> los grandes del, tomo a Mosen Suarez por la mano, e lo asento
25 cabo si, diçiendo que si el non toviera fijo legitimo, que a el heredara en el Reyno

[fol. 24r]

1 el luego mando embiar por una fija suya bastarda que ay estava, y lo caso co<n> ella
2 y lo fizo su Almirante, y la heredo en su Reyno. Pasados cuatro, o çinco dias que
3 yo estuve en la posada del Almiralle Mosen Suarez el Cardenal embio por mi
4 e me dixo, que fuese a oyr misa con el Rey, e quel me daria aviamiento para el
5 camino de Babylonia, e comeria con el. E despues de oyda misa el Rey se aparto
6 a un canto de la yglesia co<n> el Cardenal, e co<n> su tia, e co<n> algunos de su consejo,
7 e el Cardenal me dixo de parte del Rey como avia sabido que yo queria yr a
8 Babylonia a al mo<n>te de Synay, e por quanto el Rey avia de embiar un em-
9 baxador sobre fechos suyos al Solda<n>, que me rogava que yo açeptase aquello, e
10 que echaria grant cargo al Rey en ello. E yo bien conosçi quel Cardenal
11 avie tenido aquella manera por lo que a mi cumplie. E respondi que era mu-
12 cho co<n>tento de le servir por ser Rey, y Xpiano, y de la naçion de França. El
13 Rey me mando comer alli con el e co<n> el Cardenal, e alli se dio orde<n> a mi camino,
14 e dende me parti al (72) puerto de Bafa, donde el Rey tenia mandado que yo fuese
15 aposentado en un aldea ençima de una montaña que es lugar sano por la
16 gran dolentia de Bafa, e pose en casa de Diego Thenorio escudero castellano, e
17 ove mucho plaçer con el, e a cabo de tres dias llego una fusta de diez e ocho Vancos
18 al puerto de Bafa la que me avie de levar, e traye al Trujama<n> del Rey que se

19 fuese conmigo, e muchas vituallas como de casa de Rey, e las provisiones de aquello
20 que avie de façer co<n> el Soldan. El segundo dia feçimos vela e andovimos por la
21 mar onçe dias a las veçes co<n> buen viento finalme<n>te llegamos al puerto de Dami-
22 ata, donde el rio Nilo que proçede de Parayso terrenal entra en el mar Me-
23 diterraneo, e alli entramos por la rivera fasta la cibdat de Damiata, q<ue>
24 es legua, e media, que sera tamaña como Salamanca abundosa de pan
25 e de uvas, e de toda fruta, y mas de açucarales cibdat llana, y desmu-

[fol. 24v]

1 rada, y sin castillo muy caliente en demasiada manera posadas muy frescas, tan-
2 tas comadrejas por las calles y por las casas, que ay mas que aca en las partes
3 donde ay muchos ratones. Alli vi las primeras palomas, que traen la carta en
4 una pluma de la cola, esto se façe lleva<n>dolas del lugar donde so<n> cria(73)das, a
5 otra parte, e poniendole la carta suelta<n>la e tornase a su lugar esto se faze por
6 saber presto las nuevas de las gentes que viene<n> por la mar o por la tierra que
7 no<n> les tomen desproveydos pues vive<n> sin fortalezas, e sin muro. Luego como llegue
8 fuy levado al Adelantado, e dixele como yva al Soldan, e que me ma<n>dase dar
9 fusta en que fuese, que la mia no era para navegar por agua duçe, e el mandome
10 aposentar en su casa en tanto que se dava recabdo. E estando alli viniero<n> ciertos mo-
11 ros diçiendo que yo era Catalan que me avian visto comer co<n> el señor de Cande-
12 lor, e que lo querian provar. E trujero<n> dos turcos gentiles ombres que alli estava<n>
13 que dixesen la verdat. E ellos viniero<n> a mi, e viero<n>me, e dixero<n> que los moros min-
14 tien. E yo pregu<n>te si otra cosa dixiera<n> los turcos que se fiçiera de mi, dixeron que
15 la muerte, que toda cosa que los Turcos diçen es aprovada por verdat. Este lugar lle-
16 va mas datiles que parte del mundo. El Rio Nilo que por ella pasa que es uno de
17 dos braços, que se parten a una jornada de Babylonia, en el mes de Setiembre al
18 tiempo que yo estava alli creçe una vez e finche toda la tierra, e con la gra<n>de agua

19 entra<n> muchos pescados de la mar por la ribera, e allegan (74) fasta las casas. E como

20 por la grant calor las mas de las casas tiene<n> puertas a la ribera por resçebir el

21 agua, a las veçes grandes pescados entran por aquellas puertas, e encallan

22 en tierra, e alli los matan. Ay en esta ribera unas bestias que se crian de<n>tro del agua

23 que llaman cocatriz Las quales qua<n>do estan en el agua non ay ome ni bestia q<ue>

24 puedan alcançar que no<n> la matan, e diçen que fuyen en el agua del bufano

25 y por esto como en todas aquellas partes no<n> ay pue<n>te nin se podrie façer por las

[fol. 25r]

1 grandes arenas, y para aver de pasar de la una parte a la otra la pobre gente avria menes-

2 ter del alquilar barco, suben en aquellos bufanos, e pasa<n> seguros el rio a na-

3 do sin peligro ninguno. Estas bestias suelen salir fuera del agua, çinco, o

4 seys pasos, e quando façe sol estan mucho adormeçidas, e los que las van a ma-

5 tar, llevan un asta de lança e en cabo un rallon co<n> orejas que qua<n>do entra

6 aprieta, e al tirar afierra en la carne e al cabo del esta una cuerda atada, en que

7 ay çiento, e çincuenta braças, o mas, e como allega a ella si la puede ferir debaxo

8 del costado, que en otra parte no aprovecharia, entra el fierro, e alli tiene el cuero

9 muy sotil, e como se siente ferida vase al agua, e da<n>le cuerda fasta (75) tanto q<ue> anda

10 cansada, e despues tira<n>la en tierra e lleva<n>la por las villas, e lugares, dema<n>dan-

11 do como façen en Castilla el que mata el lobo. Esta es en todo fechura de lagarto

12 tienen los dientes macho, e fembra arriba, e abaxo, e por esto diçen que qua<n>do

13 travan de alguna cosa, no<n> puede<n> soltar tan ayna. Estas fuyen en la tierra de qual-

14 quier cosa, por aquella les es estraña. Destas vi muchas yo por esta ribera. Di-

15 çen muchos yo non lo vi que en esta mesma ribera se crian otras bestias que so<n> cava-

16 llos ni mas ni menos salvo que lo de la boca tiene<n> tan ancha como lo de la frente

17 e salen pegado co<n> el agua a paçer, e alli les arman unos hoyos cubiertos como lla-

18 man en Castilla loberas, e alli los matan, e estos nin en el agua, nin fuera della

19 non façen mal. Esta agua desta ribera es la mejor que yo falle bien pares-
20 çe agua de parayso En el tiempo que yo alli estuve jamas no<n> bevi sino desta
21 agua pudiendo bever buen vino. Aqui en este lugar ay tantas de codorniçes
22 que a la manera de Castilla darian diez por un maravedi, e matanlas co<n> los po-
23 dencos que las paran con un palo con dos o tres cascabeles en el cabo. Aqui folgue
24 ocho dias despues el Adelantado me fizo dar un navio para yr a Babylo(76)nia
25 que llaman Gerba que son tan luengos como una grant galea, e todo fecho de ca-

[fol. 25v]

1 maras de un cabo, e otro aposentamiento, e llanos de carena, porque nad-
2 en en poca agua, lleva<n> grandes cargos traen la vela tan alta como una carra-
3 ca salvo que es angosta, e latina como de galea E muchas veçes acaesçe en el
4 tiempo de la cresçiente del rio yr a vela e a remos e no<n> poder yr un paso adela<n>te
5 si non buscan algunt remanso, o echan la gente en tierra para que la remolquen
6 con las cuerdas luengas Llevan co<n>tinuame<n>te tres atabales uno a popa, e otro a proa
7 e otro a mediania por despantar los catrizes que dixe ninguno non osa tomar del
8 agua del rio con su mano, syno ata la vasija en un asta, e asy tiran el agua. Des-
9 pues que parti de Damiata co<n>tinuando mi camino por la ribera arriba toda la
10 fallava de una parte, e de la otra poblada de aldeas juntas co<n> el agua, e fuy a
11 aquel lugar donde se apartan los braços este por donde yo yva, e el otro que va
12 çerca de Alixandria. Ay una generaçion de gentes en Babylonia que se rapan la
13 cabeça, e las barvas e las cejas, las pestañas, e muestranse bivir como locos di-
14 çiendo que aquella es la santidat e que por serviçio de Dios despreçian el (77) mu<n>-
15 do, e su pompa que es aquella que se raparon E algunos van cargados de cuernos
16 e otros enmelados, e emplumados, e otros con unas lanzas en lanternas encendi-
17 das co<n> lumbre colgadas dellas. E otros con arcos puesta la flecha en la cuerda, e
18 asy en diversas maneras diçiendo que andan persiguiendo a los xpianos, e a

19 estos façen gran reverençia los moros. E un dia falle una flota dellos, e pregu<n>-
20 te donde yva<n>, e dixero<n>me que a meterse en u<n> fuego co<n> los perros de los xpianos
21 e ver quien se quemaria. En esta ysla que dixe de Alexandria se façen muchos
22 linos donde se façen los lienços tan buenos. E de alli continuando nuestro camino
23 en syete dias fuemos en Babylonia, e desembarcamos al puerto donde esta una
24 alhondiga, donde se allegan los xpianos, e sacamos todo lo nuestro del navio
25 e aquella noche reposamos en aquella casa. Otro dia de mañana fiçe alquilar

[fol. 26r]

1 asnos muy bien aderescados con sus sillas, e frenos muy bien andariegos, e ombre
2 que nos guiase a casa del Trujaman mayor del Soldan, e tovimos que andar des-
3 de en amanesçiendo fasta medio dia a su casa. E como llegamos a el, dile las letras
4 e saludos del Rey de Chipre e mas duçientos ducados que el Rey le embiava (78)
5 que su padre ansi ge lo dexo mandado para en toda su vida por el serviçio que le
6 fiço en la presion el qual nos resçibio mucho bien, e aposento dentro en su casa.
7 E estuve alli dos dias antes que viese al Soldan, e en estos dos dias fablando el
8 Trujaman comigo muchas cosas, e preguntandome donde era ovo de saber de mi
9 como yo era Castellano natural de Sevilla, e el huvo mucho plaçer comigo,
10 porque ansy mesmo el era de Sevilla, que seyendo niño fue levado a Ie-
11 rusalem co<n> su padre que era Judio e murio el padre, e el tornose Moro, e
12 primerame<n>te le llamavan Haym, e aora Saym, el quiso saber de mi quien
13 yo era, e como Venia, e yo non le encobri nada de mi fecho por me aprovechar
14 del, e de su consejo, e ansi lo fizo. Yo fui tan bien tratado del en su ca[sa,] dexando-
15 me andar entre sus mujeres, e fijos, como si fuera fijo propio, e diçieme que
16 esta era la mayor onrra que el me pudie façer, e que bien parescia, que yo
17 era de su naçion pues sus fijos tanto me querian. Serie este ombre de noven-
18 ta años mas por eso no dexava de façer generaçion, que aun estando yo alli le

19 pario una de sus mugeres un fijo. Este tenia quatro mugeres xpianas de a-
20 quellas que compran en la mar Mayor por quanto (79) avrien por grant desonrra
21 casar con mora de natura. Estos tres dias estuve co<n> el sin ver al Soldan
22 me mostro muchas cosas tales, y tantas que serie largo de escrevir. El ter-
23 çero dia me tomo las letras que yo traya para el soldan e se las levo, e mos-
24 tro, e ovieron consejo sobre la respuesta, e trujome esa noche las letras
25 mesmas cerradas e dixome que por yo ser su natural me queria avisar que

[fol. 26v]

1 aquellas letras las avia visto el Soldan, e que ellos tenian por mengua non
2 responder subito, e que por eso acostumbrava<n> ver primero, e que yo propusiese mi
3 fecho non dando a entender que de aquello fuese avisado. Otro dia de mañana ma<n>-
4 do tener prestas las bestias para mi e para los mios, en saliendo el sol fuemos a la
5 casa del Soldan e antes que llegasemos, por las calles yvamos comiendo, e bevie<n>do
6 que anda<n> ombres co<n> las coçinas a cuestas aparejado el comer, otros vendiendo frutas
7 otros vendiendo agua, e otros otras cosas. Llegamos a la mezquita mayor que es una
8 buena cosa de ver, pero muchas mejores he visto en tierra de xpianos, despues lle-
9 gamos a una grant plaça donde estava muy mucha gente a cavallo e çiertas tien-
10 das armadas diçen y fuera de la cibdat asy mesmo muy mucha gente a (80) cavallo,
11 por quanto aquel dia era el de la salva que se faze al Soldan e si yo non fabla-
12 re en el numero de la gente, asi a cavallo como a pie, dexolo por non deçir cosa que
13 sea dura de creer, aunque çiertame<n>te toda cosa en esta parte se puede deçir, e creer.
14 E llegamos a la puerta de la posada del Soldan, e alli dexamos las bestias, e
15 subimos por gradas fasta la puerta Esta posada sera tan grande como Villareal
16 e yendo por las calles, veya muchas gentes de una parte, e de otra, e dixieronme
17 que aquellos son los mamalucos, que aca llamamos elches renegados, una grant
18 muchedumbre de gente, e estos son los que el Soldan façe comprar por sus dineros en

19 el mar mayor, e en todas las provinçias donde los xpianos se venden E como los
20 traen alli tornan los moros, e muestranles la ley, e a cavalgar, e jugar con el arco
21 e de que son examinados por el Alfaqui mayor pone<n>les su quitaçion, e raçion, e em-
22 bianlos a la cibdat Non puede ser Soldan, nin almirante, nin aver honor ninguna
23 ni ofiçio si no es destos renegados, nin puede cavalgar moro de natura
24 sin que mueran por ello. Estos son los que han todas las onrras de la cavalleria, e
25 sus fijos un poco menos, e los nietos menos, e dende (81) adela<n>te queda<n> moros de natura

[fol. 27r]

1 esto por augmentar su ley, e por esto le llaman acresçentador de la ley de Ma-
2 homad, las fembras non tiene<n> esta prerogativa, pero antes resçebiria un Moro
3 una xpiana sin dote que una mora por bien dotada que sea mayorme<n>te
4 si es moro de natura. Yendo todavia por aquellas calles llegamos a una gra<n>t
5 puerta, que estava çerrada, e abrieronnos, e entramos dentro, e fallamos una
6 grant plaça llena de cavalleros puestos en orden arrimados a las paredes,
7 e de alli abrieron nos otra puerta, e fallamos una quadra asi mesmo en a-
8 quella orden de cavalleros. Despues abrieron nos otra puerta, e fallamos otra
9 quadra asi mesmo en aquella orden salvo que era de negros con porras e<n> las manos
10 E alli el Trujaman mayor me fizo quedar co<n> los mios fasta que bolviese a
11 mi, e a poca de ora bolvio a mi, e metiome por una puerta a una gra<n>t plaça
12 a donde estava<n> muchos cavalleros en la orde<n> que dixe, e en mitad de la plaça
13 estava una grande, e rica tienda con sus estrados do avia de comer el Soldan
14 e le avian de façer la salva, e cerca de alli estava armado un pavellon portal
15 do estava armado un cadahalso alto, e una silla, donde el Solda<n> avia de desca-
16 valgar. E el (82) Trujaman mayor me dixo, que yo esperase en mitad de aquella
17 plaça, quel Soldan saldria, e pasaria junto comigo, e que yo no<n> le feçiese re-
18 verencia ninguna, porque aquello acostumbra<n> ellos por desde<n> de los Xpianos.

19 E estando asi, abriero<n> una puerta grande, e salio el Soldan a cavallo, e dela<n>-
20 del su fijo a pie co<n> fasta doçientos cavalleros, e paso asy cerca de mi, e fuese
21 a sentar en aquella silla que dixe. Avie pocos dias quel el Solda<n> avia ma<n>dado
22 soltar de la presion un fijo del tesorero del Solda<n> aquie<n> el avie suçedido
23 el qual avie avido una grant suma de riqueza, asi en oro como en perlas
24 e piedras, e otras cosas de valor, e que para aquella fiesta por le servir e tor-

[fol. 27v]

1 nar en su graçia, le embio un cavallo de color morzillo ferrado de oro con el freno
2 e silla asi mesmo de oro guarnido, en el arçon delantero de la silla un ballax que
3 diçen que pesava un rotulo, e medio que pareçia tan grande como una naranja media-
4 na, e en el arço<n> de tras tres balajes tan gruessos como huevos de gallinas, e una çimi-
5 tarra, que valie una grant suma de oro E su Ropa era de damasco blanco por corta-
6 pisa un cerco de ricas perlas. El Trujama<n> mayor vino por mi, e dixome que fiçiese
7 muestra de besar la tierra ante que (83) llegase a el, e tomo las cartas que yo tenia e
8 pusomelas en la cabeça e en la boca por salva, e diogelas al Soldan e puesto que las
9 letras yvan en otra lengua el las leyo en lengua turca, porque delante el Soldan, nin
10 en su corte no<n> se fabla otra lengua. Diçen que esto se fizo quando el Turco tomo la
11 ley de Mahomad, que a poco tiempo, e que por la onrra le façen esta cirimonia. El
12 Soldan me pregunto por el Rey de Chipre, e por el Cardenal su tio, e por mosen Su-
13 arez, e por algunos del Reyno, e como yo le respondi luego me dixo que aquello por q<ue>
14 vinia le plaçie de façer. Esto era quel Rey le embiava a suplicar que no le embiase
15 aquellos mamalucos que le solie embiar cada año por tributo porque le façen
16 muy grant costa, e que el gelo embiaria dende en quatro meses, lo otro, que lo resçi-
17 biese en chamelotes al preçio como Valien en Babylonia Lo otro que le dexase Ven-
18 der su sal, que es una grant renta en toda la Siria sin pagar derechos, e todo se libro.
19 El Soldan luego mando que me aposentasen bien, e me diese<n> las cosas necessarias, e asi

20 me fiço. Este dia me dio el Soldan una ropa que el suele dar en señal de Vasallaje al

21 Rey de Chipre la qual era de açitimi verde, e colorado labrada de oro (84) e ferradas las

22 muestras de armiños, luego, el Soldan deçendio de aquella villa a la tienda, e alli le fiçi-

23 eron la salva e le diero<n> de comer, e alli me despedi del por este dia. E estando asi entra-

24 ron fasta çient ombres, que trayan un moro en los ombros, e pusiero<n>lo en tierra, e fue

[fol. 28r]

1 luego desnudo e dados doçientos açotes con vergas en barriga, e en espaldas E diçen

2 que toda la justiçia criminal se façe delante el Soldan. E bolvimos por aquel mes-

3 mo lugar, e no<n> fallamos ninguno de quantos a la yda aviamos visto salvo los negros

4 e desque deçendimos a la plaça grande cavalgamos en n<uest>ras bestias, e no<n> fallamos

5 en aquella plaça cavalleros, nin las tiendas salvo ombres pobres con harneros

6 ahechando las arenas, e yo pregunte que era aquello Respondiome que eran om-

7 bres de la ventura, que busca<n> alguna cosa si se caeria en el suelo de tanta muche-

8 dumbre de gente como alli se llego Este dia tovimos que andar fasta puesto el sol

9 en bolver a la posada. Otro dia reposamos, e yo ordene de embiar el desempacho del Sol-

10 dan al Rey de Chipre en aquella fusta suya que quedava en Damiata, e que vini-

11 ese dende a dos meses por mi por quanto yo entendia yr a Santa Catalina al monte de

12 Synay. (85) E despues que embie el despacho al Rey de Chipre yo estuve en Babylonia

13 çerca de un mes mirando muchas cosas, y muy estrañas mayorme<n>te a los de n<uest>ra na-

14 çion, e çiertame<n>te yo ove grant dicha en aver tal guia como aquella del Trujaman

15 mayor, quel avie grant plaçer en trabajar comigo en aquello que yo queria [....]

[fol. 31r] {14}

14 [. . . . .] Yo fui por la costa del mar berme-

15 jo, que es media legua del mo<n>te de Synay por ver como vinia la caravana, e falle

16 que vinia alli un veneçiano que deçian Nicolo de Conto gentil ombre de natura

17 e traya consigo su muger, e dos fij[o]s, e una fija que ovo en la India, e vinia el e ellos

18 tornados moros, que los fiçieron renegar en la Meca que es su casa santa, e el como

19 me vido llegose a mi e preguntome quien era, e que façia alli, e que arte era la mia,

20 e yo le dixe como era de Ytalia, e me avia criado co<n> el Rey de Chipre, e que avia

21 venido a Babilonia por su mandado al Soldan, e co<n> su licençia avia Venido alli

22 e aun entendia pasar en la India. E luego me respondio que no<n> lo devia façer E pues-

23 to que facerlo quisiese, que non lo podria acabar, e yo todavia porfiando de yr alla

24 el me dixo, e conjuro que le dixiese quien yo era, e quel me faria un gra<n>t serviçio

25 esto era, que me diria la manera (96) que avia de tener, e que bien me podia fiar del

[fol. 31v]

1 pues que el xpiano era como yo, e quel me co<n>taria el proçeso de su vida, e como

2 era venido alli. E yo mirando como era persona grave e discreta, e de bue<n> gesto

3 dixele como yo era fidalgo, e cavallero natural despaña, e como vine al Santo

4 Sepulcro, e de alli a Babylonia con entençion de venir al monte de Synay, e de

5 alli pasar a la India. [. . . . .]

[fol. 38v] {18}

18 [. . . . .] e quando lo

19 ove bien visto partime por tierra e fui a Damiata, e no<n> falle a mi fusta quel

20 Rey de Chipre me avia dado e esperela ocho dias, e vino que era yda façia la

21 costa de Jerusalem, e alli resçebi muncha honrra del Adelantado que le traya car-

22 tas del Trujaman mayor del Soldan de recomendaçion para mi, e embiole a ro-

23 gar que si tenia algunt cuero de cocatriz, que embiase al Rey de Chypre que le

24 avie a rogar e ofresçiose que avian muerto una, e estava fresca, e olie muy mal, tanto

[fol. 39r]

1 que mejor fuera aver traydo una fija del Adelantado muy fermosa quel alli
2 tenie, quel cuero de cocatriz, e metime a la mar e en siete dias arribe al pu-
3 erto de Bafa, do avia embarcado lugar muy doliente, e aun aquel dia que lle-
4 gue avia finado el Obispo, e dos escuderos suyos, e fiçome Dios mercet que en
5 poniendo el pie en tierra luego en las bestias del Obispo e los suyos caval-
6 gue, (120) e me parti para la corte del Rey de Chipre que estava en Nicosia e mi
7 Truxaman quel Rey me avia dado fue delante a lo deçir al Rey e al Cardenal
8 e embiaronme mandar que me detuviese aquella noche en un aldea porque otro
9 dia de mañana me querien façer resçebir honorableme<n>te, e a<n>sy lo feçiero<n>, otro dia
10 de mañana yendo por mi camino falle muchos de aquellos señores de la corte
11 del Rey que me salien a resçebir e me acompañaro<n> fasta la persona del Rey, e
12 quando llegue falle al Rey e al Cardenal, e muchos de los grandes con ellos
13 e fue mucho bien resçebido, e con tanta humanidat tratado como si yo fuera
14 su natural, e agradesçiendo a Dios como yo era tornado a salvame<n>to de tan
15 grant viaje E regradesçiendome mucho de parte del Rey lo que yo avia fecho
16 en su serviçio, e porferiendome mucho las cosas que me pluguiesen. E en esto
17 despedime del Rey E el Almirante que alli estava, llevome a su posada co-
18 mo solia, donde fuy muy bien ospedado. Otro dia de mañana levantose un
19 grant rumor en todo el pueblo, e todos se posieron en armas, el Cardenal prin-
20 çipalmente, e Madama Ynes su hermana, e algunos de los grandes del Rey-
21 no contra el Rey por le matar, o prender un privado (121) que llamava<n>
22 Iacobo Guiri, e por ofiçio auditor. El Rey fuyo a una fortaleça que esta en
23 cabo de la çibdat, que llaman la Cibdadel, e alli lo çercaron, e tovieron tal par-
24 tido con el, que echase de si el privado, e que no<n> entrase en su corte por un año
25 e ansy lo juro el Rey, e luego se cumplio, e levantaronse de sobrel. Otro dia

[fol. 39v]

1 siguiente el Rey embio por mi, e delante el Cardenal, e algunos nobles me
2 dixo, e rogo que tomase del lo que me pluguiese para la costa de mi camino,
3 e yo respondi, que ge lo tenia en mucha merçed, que yo tenia asaz para mi buelta, e
4 que le suplicava que me mandase dar licençia, e una fusta que me levase fas-
5 ta Rodas, e yo trabajava quanto podia por me partir, e el por me detener, e man-
6 dome que estoviese alli a lo menos ocho dias, e yo porque vi que avia el plaçer
7 ovelo de facer, y sin duda en estos dias yo fuy tam bien refrescado que mejor no<n>
8 podia ser, e aderesçose el navio que me avia de levar, e despedime del Rey, e çier-
9 tamente de mala voluntad me dava la licençia, e alli me dio su devisa que oy
10 tengo, e me dio diez piezas de chamelote, e lienços delgados, e un leon pardo
11 e tantas vituallas para yr fasta Rodas, que bastaran para un año. E en este
12 tiempo (122) que alli estuve viniero<n> dos embaxadas al rey de Chipre una del
13 duque de Saboya, e otra de un duque de Alemaña por contraer casamien-
14 to cada uno dellos con su fija, e yo non dexe conclusion fecha con ninguno de-
15 llos, porque se diçia que otro casamiento le traya el Maestre de Rodas muy
16 afincado con una fija del conde de Urgel de Aragon hermana de la muger
17 del infante Don Pedro Rigente de Portogal Pero pareçiome que a lo que
18 mas deliñavan los del consejo del rey era con la fija del duque de Saboya,
19 e creo que esto huvo conclusion. El Rey era mozo de diez e seys o diez e siete a-
20 ños, e grande de persona aunque las perinas por el jarrete sin dubda ninguna
21 tenia tan gruessas como poco menos por el muslo graçioso ombre, e para se hedat asaz
22 de buen engenio, e ombre alegre, e dispuesto del cuerpo mayorme<n>te en el cavalgar
23 e sin dubda si la tierra non fuera tan mal sana de buena voluntad me dis-
24 pusiera a le servir alguna temporada mas fuera quasi imposible poder bivir
25 en tierra tan doliente ombre estrangero, e por eso, e por el deseo que tenia de bolver

[fol. 40r]

1 en Castilla, por cabsa de la guerra de los moros ove de continuar mi camino

2 lo mas presto que yo pude.

3 [. . . . .]

4 (123) Parti de la cibdat de Nicosia, e fuy a Atherines, do me esperava el navio que

5 me avia de levar a Rodas, e esta es una cibdat antigua que fiço Archiles, e de

6 alli ovo el nombre pequeña cibdat pero fuerte, e bien murada, e buen puerto

7 aunque pequeño pero encadenado e bien guardado, aqui escapo el Rey que a-

8 gora es, e el Cardenal su tio, e Madama Ynes, e otros muchos del reyno qua\<n\>do

9 el Rey Ianus fue preso Esta es la mas sana tierra que ay en todo el Reyno de

10 Chipre, porque es decubierta a viento poniente. E alli falle presto un Gr[i]-

11 po que el Rey me avia mandado aparejar para que me levase a Rodas, e

12 otro Gripo estava con el en compañia que levava mercaduria. E salimos del

13 puerto, e fuemos a la punta del cabo de San Pifani, e alli estuvimos fasta

14 medio dia e fecimos vela, e metimonos a la mar por el golfo de Satalias la via

15 de la Turquia e antes de dos oras vimos venir una galea de Turcos que venia

16 contra nosotros por nos tomar e despedaçar por una fusta que los catalanes avi-

17 an tomado de Turcos sobre el puerto de Chipre, e nosotros a vela e a remos, e

18 ellos ansy mesmo tanto que alli no falleçia la letania las manos bien trabaja-

19 das de remar. Yva comigo un comitre (124) de una galea de catalanes, que avie muerto a

20 un sobrino del patron, y mandolo aforcar del entena, e quebrose la soga co\<n\> el

21 e yo roguele tanto que me lo diese pues Dios avie fecho tanto por el, e plugole

22 e por esto escapamos que sabia mucho de navegar, fiço aliviar el peso que le-

23 vava n\<uest\>ro Gripo para que mejor caminase, e el otro de mercadurias no quiso echar

24 lo a la mar e quando ya era tarde, quel sol se querie poner los Turcos al-

25 cançaron, e anegaronlos a todos, e en el embaraço que fiçiero\<n\> con ellos, ovimos

[fol. 40v]

1 tiempo de alargarnos un poco, e quando quiso anocheçer guindamos la vela qua<n>-
2 to podimos, e todos tomamos mano a los remos, e trabajamos media ora qua<n>-
3 to en el mundo podimos, e quanto fue la noche escuro calamos la vela, e toma-
4 mos a la mano derecha bogando muy quedo, que non sonasen los remos, e la ga-
5 lea paso bien çerca de nosotros que no nos vido. El comitre catalan dixo que
6 convenia facer otro mejor mareaje que la galea tomaria la buelta de la tierra
7 esperando como era navio pequeño el nuestro, e que nos avrien a las manos
8 E tomamos la buelta de la mar, e la galea vimosla yr façia la tierra, e a media
9 noche salto un viento a la mar de Mediodia que cada (125) onda nos envistie de Va<n>da
10 a Vanda, quanto yo mas quisiera aver caydo en poder de los Turcos que non ser
11 anegado en tal lugar. Alli me querian echar un ombre mio a la mar salvo q<ue>
12 lo defendimos muy bien. Con esta fortuna corrimos fasta Castilrroxo, e allegamos
13 a ora de terçia, e la galea avia partido de ay non avrie dos oras. Deçendimos en tier-
14 ra que es un buen puerto e subimos arriba que es una grant fortaleza, e alli
15 reposamos como quien escapa de una grant dolençia. Este castillo es de la reli-
16 gion de Rodas es de la Provinçia de Armenia aunque es ysla, e es tan enrroca-
17 do que ninguna bestia non puede subir arriba, e abaxo a la entrada del Puerto
18 tiene unas salinas que son de grant renta de los cavalleros de Rodas.
19 [. . . . .]
20 Partimos de la ysla de Castilroxo façiendo el camino de Rodas con grant mie-
21 do de aquella galea, e ovimos mal tiempo en la mar Pero en dos dias de cami-
22 no llegamos a Rodas, e entramos en el puerto, e luego me fuy a posar con frey
23 Nuño de Cabrera un buen cavallero natural n<uest>ro de Castilla, e de la religion,
24 e aun de los que alla mas (126) cabdal tenian, e aun mas mençion se façia, el qual muy
25 alegre e amorosame<n>te me resçibio, e tan humaname<n>te fuy del tratado que yo me

[fol. 41r]

1 pensava morir segunt el trabajo que avia pasado syno fuera por por la buena co<m>-
2 pañia que me fiço, que non pudiera yo en mi casa propia ser mas piadosame<n>-
3 te, nin mejor servido. El segundo dia que llegue ove de yr al Maestre de Rodas
4 a le dar çiertas letras del rey de Chipre de negocios suyos, que me avia encomenda-
5 do, e acompañaronme frey Nuño de Cabrera, e otros cavalleros Castellanos, e
6 aun de otras naçiones espeçialme<n>te los françeses que se llegan mucho con n<uest>ra naçio<n>
7 E como llegue al Maestre fallelo muy agraviado de dolor de la yjada pero luego des-
8 pacho la respuesta del rey de Chipre e partime del, e bolvi a la posada, e aquella
9 noche murio del aquel mal. [. . . . .]

[fol. 65r]   {3}

3 [. . . . .] Las casas desta çibdat son muy nota-
4 bles e muy altas muy encamaradas, e co<n> muchas chimeneas, e preçianse de ricas
5 portadas, e finiestras a las calles labradas ricame<n>te de oro, y de açul bien enmarmo-
6 ladas, e ay señores en torno, e aun lexos de alli que se preçian de se aveçindar en la
7 çibdat, por tal de aver su favor quando menester les fuere, asi como el rey de Chipre,
8 el Marques de Ferrara, el Marques de Mantua, el marques de Monferrat e otros
9 muchos señores, e cavalleros tiene<n> alli muy magnificas casas. Yo vi al cardenal de
10 Chipre, hermano del Rey, que posava alli en casa de su hermano, e que se queria
11 partir para Chipre, e la galea que lo avia de llevar estava atada a la (210) puerta de su
12 casa, e alli lo resçibio, e salio con el por la meytad de la çibdat, e asy otros
13 navios grandes, e medianos se amarran a las puertas de sus señores. [. . . . .]

Appendix 2

Monstrelet on the Capture of King Janus of Cyprus

CHAPITRE XXXIX

Comment les Sarrasins retournèrent en Chipre et eurent bataille aux Chipriens, en laquelle bataille le roy fu prins et mené au Soudant.

En ce temps arrivèrent devers le roy de Cyppre plusieurs chevaliers et escuyers de divers pays, lesquelx par avant avoit mandés pour résister contre l'armée des Sarrasins que chascun jour il attendoit. Et avec ce assambla de son royaume ce qu'il peut avoir de gens, auxquelx il pourveut de vivres, logis et argent, au mieulx qu'il peut, chascun selon son estat. Et entretant qu'il attendoit, comme dit est, la venue des Sarrasins, ses gens qui estoient de diverses nacions s'esmeurent par plusieurs fois l'un contre l'autre, par telle manière que le roy avoit assez à faire à mettre paix entre eulx, et ne sçavoit comment il peust ordonner capitaine qui à ceulx fust agréable. Durant lesquelles divisions les Sarrasins arrivèrent ou royaume de Cyppre en très grand multitude, et prinrent port à Lymeçon et assiégièrent la tour, qui estoit très bien réparée et garnie de gens d'armes. Mais non obstant elle fut prinse par force, et le capitaine, nommé Estievene de Buiseuses, mort avec toutes ses gens.

Et adonc le roy de Cyppre, sachant les nouvelles de ses ennemis, assambla ceulx de son conseil et leur demanda qu'il en avoit à faire. Et la plus grand partie de ceulx de son pays lui firent responce, qu'il se tenist en sa ville de Nicosie, disant que mieulx valoit pays gasté que perdu. Mais tous les estrangiers furent de contraire opinion et lui conseillèrent qu'il se meist aux champs et qu'il combatist bien et hardiement ses ennemis, lesquelx destruisoient ainsy son pays et mettoient à mort cruelle son povre peuple. Le roy ce oyant, délibéra soy mettre aux champs le second jour ensuivant. Et quand le jour vint et qu'il monta à cheval, le premier pas que son destrier fist il s'agenoulla jusques à terre, et le prince de Galilée son frère, en montant à cheval, laissa cheoir son espée hors du fourrel à terre. Dont plusieurs eurent petite espérance qu'ilz deussent avoir victoire.

Et ala, celui jour, le roy loger à trois lieues près de la cité, en une place moult délitable nommée Biau Lieu, et le samedi ensuivant, dont c'estoit le jeudi, chevaulcha en belle ordonnance jusques à une ville nommée Cytocie. Et le dimenche ensuivant vi jour de jullet, après que le roy ot oy ses messes, il se assist à table, et à celle heure que lui et tous ceulx de son ost disnoient, fut veu en plusieurs lieux grand fumée des feux que les Sarrasins boutoient, et lors furent au roy apportées certaines nouvelles qu'ilz venoient contre luy. Et adonc le Grand commandeur de Cyppre, avec plusieurs frères de Rodes de sa religion, et aussy le seigneur de Varembolois, alemant, et aucuns autres gentilz hommes de la nacion de France, demandèrent au roy congié d'aler descouvrir et veoir leurs ennemis. Lequel leur accorda, moult envis. Si alèrent si avant qu'ilz trouvèrent les Sarrasins, auxquelz ilz escarmuchèrent et en occirent aucuns. Mais en fin, pour la très grande habondance d'yceulx ilz ne porent porter la charge, et en y eut de mors trente ou environ, et les autres se retrayrent envers le roy au mieulx que faire le porrent. Lequel roy chevauchoit grant oire pour trouver ses ennemis.

Et ainsi sans faire grande ordonnance chevaucha grande espace, et tant qu'il trouva le Sarrasins assez près d'une ville qui s'appelle Domy. Et estoient au plus près de lui, son frère, prince de Galilée, le connestable de Jhérusalem, deux contes d'Alemaigne et toute la fleur de sa chevalerie. Et adonc le dessusdit roy de Cyppre assailli moult chevaleuresement et soubdainement les Sarrasins, ses adversaires, et tant que de plaine venue leur fist très grand dommage. Mais, ainsy que fortune le volt adverser, le coursier du roy chey des quatre piés à terre, et se desclavèrent les chaingles de sa selle. Et après qu'il fut remonté et qu'il volt faire fais d'armes, la selle tourna et le roy chey à terre et son cheval s'enfuy, et fut de necessité qu'il montast sur ung petit cheval d'un sien escuyer, nommé Antoine Kairy, car tous les petis paiges s'en estoient fuys de freeur, à tout les grands coursiers. Pour laquelle adventure grant partie des Cypriens cuidèrent certainement que leur roy fust mort, et demourèrent tous esbahis. Et pour ce les Sarrasins, qui jà tournoient en fuie, reprinrent courage. Si vint leur grosse bataille, qui charga sur la gent chrestienne si puissamment, qu'il fut de necessité au roy qu'il se retrayst en la Charcottie dont il s'estoit party. Et quant il vint assez près dudit lieu, ycelui lieu estoit jà environné des Sarrasins, tellement qu'il n'y peut entrer.

Et adonc se mirent les Christiens en desroy, et commencèrent à fuyr chascun où ilz porent pour le mieulx. Le roy se retraist sur une montaignette asssez adventageuse. Et tousjours estoit au plus près de luy son frère le prince de Galilée, lequel lui dist ainsy: "Monseigneur, vous véés clèrement que toutes voz gens vous habandonnent et que vous ne povés résister contre vos ennemis, veuillez sauver vostre personne, et ayés compacion de vostre royaume. Se vous estes prins, nous sommes tous perdus. Prenés aucuns de voz plus féables serviteurs; si vous retrayés en aucune seure place, et je demourray cy avec les bannières jusques ad ce que je sentiray que vous serés en lieu seur, et puis feray pour le salut de ma personne ce qu'à Dieu plaira à moy administrer." Le roy oyant ce le regarda moult doulcement, et lui respondi: "Biau frère, jà Dieu ne plaise que je me parte. Alés reconforter et rassambler mes gens en eulx admonestant qu'à ce besoing se veullent acquiter ou service de leur souverain et natural seigneur."

Lequel prince de Galilée y ala, à telle heure qu'il fut si durement rencontré de la gent Sarazine que après qu'il eut fait tant de fais d'armes que vaillant prince povoit faire, il fut occis et là demoura mort sur la place. D'aultre part le roy fut si très fort engrossé de ses ennemis, qu'il se parti, tout habandonné de ses gens, et descendit de la montagne où il estoit, en une petiite valée, et là fut tellement assailly qu'il fut enferré en quatre lieux. Si qu'il fut abatu de son cheval à terre, et la gent Sarrasine, non congnoissant que ce fust le roy, de toutes pars commencèrent à férir sur lui pour le mettre à mort, quand ung chevalier de Castelongne du parti d'ycelui roy, nommé Gasserant Savari, se coucha sur le roy, en criant à haulte voix en langage surien: "C'est le Roy! c'est le Roy!" Adonc ung capitaine Sarrazin fist ung signe de sa main, auquel tous les autres laissèrent cheoir leurs espées à terre, et le capitaine rebouta la soie ou fourrel, et prestement s'en ala devers le roy, en lui disant en langage grec, qu'il avoit pleu à Dieu le délivrer en la main et puissance du Soudant, et lui dit: "Vous venrés pardevers luy, reconfortés vous, car pour certain j'ay bonne espérance qu'il vous fera bonne campaignie." Le dessusdit chevalier cathelan fut prins avec le roy, et luy respitèrent la vie pour ce qu'il s'estoit si vaillamment maintenu.

Ainsy et par ceste manière fut le roy de Cyppre prins de la gent Sarrazine, qui lui mirent une chaine au col. Et tantost après arrivèrent les gens de pied, qui à toute fin vouloient occire le roy. Mais Dieu par sa doulce miséricorde l'en délivra. Car il estoit homme charitable et de bonne vie envers Dieu.

Et brief ensuivant tous ceulx de la partie du roy de Cyppre furent mis à desconfiture, et se sauvèrent ceulx qui sauver se porent, et la plus grand partie par les montaignes où ilz porent le mieulx, et n'en demoura de mors en la place que environ de seize à dix sept cens. Et assez brief ensuivant la gent Sarrasine menèrent le roy de Cyppre à Salmes, où estoit leur navire, et là le mirent en bonne garde. Si furent en celle bataille devant dicte deux contes d'Allemaigne, est assavoir le conte de Hainseberghe et le conte de Noorth, advoué de Coulongne, à tout certain nombre de gens. Et si y estoient de Savoie, le seigneur de Varenbon et messire Jehan de Champaings, seigneur de Gruffy. Lesquelx dessusdiz ne furent, à ladicte bataille, ne mors ne pris.

Item, après ce qu'il fut venu à la congnoissance de par le pays de Cyppre et à Nicossie, de la desconfiture de leurs gens et de la prise de leur roy, messire Gille de Lussegnon, frère du roy, et esleu archevesque de Nicossie, avec lui messire Jaques de Caffran, mareschal de Cyppre, qui par l'ordonnance du roy estoient demourés pour la garde de ses enfants, furent adonc moult troublés et desconfortés pour ces piteuses nouvelles, et pour tant, ycelui dimenche, à heure de mie nuit, se départirent de la cité et emmenèrent avec eulx la seur du roy et ses enfants, et si le conduirent en la forteresce de Chermes, qui est située sur la mer à cincq lieues près de Nicossie, et là demourèrent jusques au retour de roy. Et lendemain, qu'il fu le lundi, la communaulté de la ville coururent au palais pour sçavoir aucunes nouvelles du roy. Et quand ilz ne trouvèrent à cuy parler, ilz retournèrent en leurs maisons et prindrent leurs femmes et leurs enfants et aucuns de leurs biens et se départirent de la ville, laissant ycelle du tout habandonnée, si non de povre gent impotente et avugle. Et s'enfuyrent les aucuns devers Famagouce, les autres à Chermes et en autres villes par les montaignes, tant que c'estoit très piteuse chose à les veoir.

Et le second jour ensuivant, le capitaine de Sarraisins ala, à tout sa gent, vers la cité de Nicossie, laquelle comme dit est il trouva du tout habandonnée. Si se loga ou palais roial et fist cryer prestement par la cité que tout homme retournast en son propre lieu, est assavoir ceulx de la ville, et on les tendroit paisibles. Pour lequel cry retournèrent dedens ladicte cité, environ de dix à douze mille personnes.

Or est vérité que le roy de Cyppre et le Grandmaistre de Rodes avoient une très grande armée sur la mer, dedens laquelle estoit le bastard de Bourgongne, frère au duc Phelippe, le seigneur de Roubaix et moult d'autres notables seigneurs de diverses marches, lesquelx estoient moult désirans de combatre les Sarrazins. Mais oncques ne peurent avoir vent propice pour eulx monstrer contre lesdiz Sarrasins. Et estoit ledit bastard de Bourgongne arrivé à Vaffe, espérant d'estre à ladicte journée. Et entretant le roy fu prins, comme dit est, et pour ce, ycelui bastard et les siens retournèrent sur mer pour de rechief aler contre yceulx Sarrazins. Et adonc le vent leva tel que les Chrestiens désiroient, et tant qu'en peu d'espace arrivèrent vers l'armée des Sarrazins, et tellement que les parties virent l'un l'autre. Et adonc le capitaine des Sarrasins, qui aussy estoit en mer, voiant les Chrestiens en grand nombre, envoia hastivement ses mesages à l'autre capitaine sarrazin qui estoit à Nicossie. Si lui manda destroitement et sur paine d'estre réputé traytre, qu'il retournast, à tout son ost et ses gens, en son navire. Laquelle chose ledit capitaine acomply. Et, après qu'il eust robé toute la cité de Nicossie et réduict le peuple en chétiveté, il fist bouter les feux ou palais royal et en plusieurs autres lieux, et s'en ala, à tout les siens, à Salmes, où estoit leur navire. Et durant le chemin prinrent plusieurs enfants alaitans leurs mere, et les gectoient sur les espines et sur les hayes, en eulx lapidant très horiblement.

Et d'autre part, le capitaine sarrazin, qui tenoit le roy de Cippre prisonnier, luy fist escripre unes lectres à son capitaine général qui estoit sur la mer, contenant, ou en substance, qu'il ne portast nul dommage aux Sarrazins, si chier qu'il avoit la vie dudit roy. Et le porta sur une petite galiotte messire Galleran Savary. Auxquelles lettres le capitaine des Chrestiens obéy, ce que faire ne debvoit seloncq l'opinion de plusieurs. Mais par avant avoient les deux parties fort approchié l'un l'autre, et y avoit eu grand besongne. A laquelle besongne, qui fu de par mer, y eut très dure escarmuche, par espécial de trait, duquel furent, tant d'un party comme d'autre, plusieurs hommes mors et navrés.

Et à celle besongne furent fais chevaliers Guy, bastard de Bourgongne, frère au duc Phelippe, Symon de Lalain, Robert, signeur de Robecque, et aucuns autres de diverses marches, sans conquerre navire l'un sur l'autre, si non la nef des pélerins, dont cy-après est faite mencion. Durant lequel temps se advança une navée chargié de pélerins voulans acquerre honneur. Et espérans pour certain que l'armée des Chrestiens qui estoit sur mer deuist combatre les Sarrazins, alèrent si avant qu'ilz ne porent retourner, et non estans secourus, furent prins, et en la présence du roy de Cyppre, coppés en pièces comme on coppe char au maisiel. Si non aucuns, en très petit nombre, qui furent retenus prisonniers. Et après aucuns peu de jours se remirent à voie, et retournèrent à tout le roy de Cyppre en Surie.

Item, quand lesdiz Sarrasins furent arrivés en Surie à tout leurs prisonniers, ilz menèrent ledit roy de Cypre au Kaire devers le Soudant de Babilonne. Et les autres Chrestiens estoient deux et deux loyés comme bestes. Et trainoient les Sarrasins après eulx la bannière Nostre-Dame, le chief en terre, et puis en après le roy de Cyppre chevauchoit sur ung petit mulet san selle, loyé et enchainé de chaines de fer. Et en cel estat fu mené en la présence du Soudant, et, constraint ad ce faire, s'agenoulla par neuf fois en enclinant le chief tout bas, baisant la terre à chascune fois. Et quand il fu parvenu jusques au Soudant, qui séoit pompeusement en une gallerie en hault, le fist estre une grosse heure ou environ en bas, en sa présence. Et depuis le fist mener en une grosse tour, où il tint prison tant qu'il fu en la ville du Kaire, où il le fist servir très habondamment, comme roy, de tous vivres, fors de vin. Mais les marchans chrestiens lui en faisoient délivrer secrètement à grand plenté. Et les autres prisonniers chrestiens furent menés en divers lieux.

Item, entretant que ledit roy de Cyppre estoit ainsy en prison au Kaire pardevant le Soudant de Babilone, l'arcevesque de Nicossie, qui estoit frère audit roy, manda messire Pierre de Lussegnen, connestable de Jhérusalem, et luy bailla le gouvernement du royaume de Cypre. Lequel fist faire de grans justices, en punissant ceulx qui s'estoient volu rebeller depuis les tribulacions dessusdictes. Et peu de temps après retourna ledit esleu en la cité de Nicossie, laquelle peu après se repeupla.

Et brief ensuivant, ung marchant genevoix, nommé Benedict Zuessin, commeu de pitié, requist au conseil du Roy qu'ilz envoiassent au Kaire, disant qu'il avoit espérance d'estre occasion de la rédempcion du Roy. Lequel y fu envoyé, et tant y exploita que le soudant mist le roi de Chippre à finance de deux cent mille ducas, par telle condicion que perpetuelment il payeroit pour chascun an trebu de son royaume, de la somme de cinq mille ducas. Et par ainsy fu la paix faite du Soudant avec le Roi de Cyppre. Et fu mis hors des fers, le jour del Assumpcion Nostre Dame. Et depuis ce, le demandoit souvent le Soudant, pour causer avec luy et luy faisoit de merveilleuses questions, en le temptant de habandonner la foy chrestienne. Aux quelles questions le roy respondi à toutes fois si sagement, que le Soudant, non sachant plus que dire, le faisoit prendre avec lui plusieurs refections de boires et de mengiers, et puis le renvoyoit en prison. Et dedans briefs jours ensuivans qu'il fu mis à finance, le fist ledit Soudant mettre hors de prison et logier dans la ville.

Et le faisoit souvent aler en estat en esbatement sur beaulx chevaulx, noblement acompaignié de la gent Sarrasine. Et depuis fut paiée grand partie de sa finance et bailliée seureté du seurplus. Et après, le jour de Pasques Flouries, fu mis à plaine délivrance. Et fu mis en une galée au port d'Alixandre sur la mer verde. A tout laquelle compaignie de l'amiral de Rodes, il ala descendre à Chermes, et là trouva ses enfans et sa seur et tous les seigneurs et dames de son royaume, avec toute la baronnie et noblesce de son pays, qui tous ensamble le receurent moult révéramment, en regraciant Nostre Seigneur très humblement de sa revenue.

Et aucuns jours ensuivans se parti de Chermes; et retourna, acompaignié comme dit est, en sa cité de Nicossie, où il fu de tout son peuple receu joieusement, et se loga en l'ostel du connestable de Jhérusalem. Ouquel hostel il demoura sa vie durant, pour ce que son palais, comme dit est dessus, avoit esté destruict de la gent Sarrazine. Et depuis le trespas de la royne Charlotte, ne fut remarié ne eut compaignie à nulle femme, comme ses propres serviteurs le tenoient véritablement. Et vesqui depuis grand espace de temps.

Appendix 3

Johnes's translation of Monstrelet

THE CHRONICLES OF ENGUERRAND DE MONSTRELET.

Chapter XXXIX.

THE SARACENS RETURN TO CYPRUS. — A BATTLE BETWEEN THEM AND THE CYPRIOTS, IN WHICH THE KING IS MADE PRISONER, AND CARRIED TO THE SULTAN.

About this period, many knights and esquires arrived at Cyprus, in consequence of the king of Cyprus's solicitations to oppose the Saracens, who were daily expected to return thither. The king collected all the forces within the island, whom he provided with lodging, food, and money, as well as he could, according to their different ranks. While they were thus expecting the Saracens, his army, which was collected from various nations, mutinied, so that the king had much difficulty to keep peace among them, and knew not whom to appoint as commander-in-chief, who would be agreeable to them. During these dissentions, the Saracens came before Cyprus in prodigious numbers, and landed at Lymeson: they besieged the great tower, and, notwithstanding it had been much strengthened, and was full of men-at-arms, they took it by storm, and killed the governor, Estienne de Buyserse, and all his men.

The king, hearing of this, assembled his council, and demanded what measures he should pursue. The greater part proposed that he should remain in the town of Nicosia, saying that a country wasted was better than a country lost; but all the foreigners were of a contrary opinion, and advised him to march his army into the plain, and combat boldly an enemy who was destroying his kingdom, and putting to death his subjects. The king, on this, determined to march his army to meet the Saracens; and on the second day after, when he was mounted, his horse, at the first step, fell on its knees to the ground. The prince of Galilee also, his brother, let his sword fall out of the scabbard on the earth: many persons thought these such omens of ill success, that they had but little hopes of victory.

This day the king advanced three leagues, and fixed his quarters at a very beautiful spot call Beaulieu. On the Saturday following, for on the Thursday he had taken the field, he marched in handsome array to a town call Citolye. On the ensuing Sunday, the 6th day of July, after the king had attended mass, and was seated at table, and while he and his army were at dinner, a great smoke was seen in different parts not far distant, and intelligence was brought that the Saracens were advancing against him. The commander of Cyprus, with some of the knights of Rhodes, the lord de Varemboulais, and several gentlemen from France, hearing this, requested the king's permission to go and reconnoitre the enemy. It was very unwillingly granted. They advanced so far that they fell in with the Saracens, with whom they skirmished, and killed a few; but numbers were so much against them that they could not longer resist, and, leaving nearly thirty dead behind them, retreated as well as they could to their army, which they met, with the king, advancing at a quick pace.

The king of Cyprus marched his army without much order for some time, and at last came in sight of the Saracens near to a town called Domy. He had near him his brother the prince of Galilee, the constable of Jerusalem, two German counts, and the flower of his own chivalry. The king charged the Saracens very gallantly and rapidly, insomuch that at the onset they suffered much; but fortune seemed unwilling to continue her favours, for the king's horse fell under him to the ground and burst the girths of the saddle; so that when the king was remounted, and engaged in the combat, the saddle turned, and he fell to the ground: the horse galloped off, and necessity forced him to mount a small horse of one of his esquires, named Anthony Kaire, for the boys had fled for fear with all the war-horses. By reason of this accident, most of the Cypriots believed their king was killed, and were panic-struck. The Saracens were beginning to retreat toward the coast, but, observing some disorder in the enemy's army, recovered their courage, and with their main body charged the Christians with such vigour that the king was obliged to retire to Citolye, whence he had departed; but when almost close to it, he was surrounded by the Saracens, and his entrance cut off.

The Christians were now discomfited, and began to fly on all sides as fast as they could. The king retired to an eminence, alway attended by his brother the prince of Galilee, who said to him, "My lord, you see clearly that your men are flying, and that all resistance against the enemy is vain: deign, therefore, to save yourself, and take compassion on your kingdom, for should you be made prisoner we shall all be ruined. Take with you therefore some of your most faithful servants, and retire to a place of safety. In the mean time, I will remain here with the banners until I shall be sure that you have escaped, and will then save myself in the manner God shall be pleased to point out to me." The king, on hearing these words, looked with much tenderness on his brother, and replied, "Fair brother, God forbid that I should separate myself from you: go, and comfort and rally my people, and urge them to the assistance of their natural lord and sovereign in his distress."

The prince of Galilee departed, but was met by a large body of Saracens, by whom, after displaying acts of valour worthy of a prince, he was slain and left dead on the field. On the other hand, the king was so hardly pressed that, finding himself abandoned by his men, he descended the eminence and made for a small valley; but he was pursued, wounded in four places, and at length struck off his horse. The Saracens, ignorant that it was the king, rushed on him from all quarters to put him to death, when a knight from Catalonia, called sir Galeran Savary, throwing himself over the king's body, cried out, in the Syrian language, "It is the king! it is the king!" upon which a Saracen captain made a sign with his hand, when all around dropped their swords to the ground, and the captain thrust his own into the scabbard. He then advanced to the king, took him by the hand, and, addressing him in Greek, said, that it had pleased God to deliver him into the hands and power of the sultan. "You will come before him; but take comfort, for I have the greatest hopes that he will be a good friend to you." The Catalonian knight was made prisoner with the king; for his life was spared on account of the great courage he had displayed. Thus was the king of Cyprus made captive by the Saracens, who fastened a chain round his neck; and shortly after, a body of Saracen infantry came up, who wanted, by all means, to put the king to death; but God, from his kind mercy, saved him, for he was a man of great charity, and of a pious life toward his God.

The army of Cyprus, after its defeat, saved itself as well as it could, and the greater part fled to the mountains: there remained dead on the field from sixteen to seventeen hundred. The Saracens carried the king to the coast, where their shipping lay, and put him under a strong guard. There were in this battle two counts from Germany, namely, the count de Humberche, and the count de Noorch, protector of Cologne, with a certain number of their vassals. There were also from Savoy, the lord de Varembon, and sir John de Champaigns lord de Gruffy,—and all these gentlemen escaped death and imprisonment.

When the news of this defeat and capture of the king was known throughout Cyprus, sir Gilles de Lusignan, brother to the king and archbishop of Nicosia, sir James de Caffran; marshal of Cyprus, who had remained as guard to the royal children, were much troubled at these melancholy events; and about midnight of this same Sunday they left the city of Nicosia, carrying with them the king's sister and his children to the castle of Cerines, on the sea-coast, about five leagues distant from Nicosia, where they remained until the king's return. On the morrow, Monday, the commonalty of the town hastened to the palace to learn some news of the king; but finding no one to speak with, they returned home, and taking their wives, children, and effects, quitted the town, leaving the whole abandoned to old beggars and blind men. Some of them fled to Famagousta, others to Cerines, to divers towns, or to the mountains, so that it was a piteous spectacle.

On the second day after the battle, the chief of the Saracens marched his army to Nicosia, which he found abandoned. He was lodged in the royal palace, and caused a proclamation to be instantly issued for all the inhabitants to return to their houses and occupations, on promise of not being disturbed, or any way molested. In consequence of this proclamation, from ten to twelve thousand persons returned to the city.

The king of Cyprus and the grand master of Rhodes had at this time a considerable fleet at sea, on board of which were, the bastard of Burgundy, brother to duke Philip, the lord de Roubaix, and many other great lords from divers countries, very impatient to combat the Saracens; but they never could have a favourable wind to carry them near the infidels. The bastard of Burgundy had arrived at Baffa, in hopes of being present at the battle in which the king was captured; but hearing of the unfortunate issue of that day, he and his men returned, and embarked again on board of the fleet. At length the Christians had a favourable wind, which brought them in a short time within sight of the enemy's fleet. The commander of the Saracens was then on board, and, seeing the Christians so numerous, sent messengers in haste to the governor of Nicosia, ordering him, on pain of being reputed a traitor, to return with his men to his ship without delay. This order he obeyed, but not until he had plundered the city of all that he could, and reduced the inhabitants to poverty. He also set fire to the royal palace, and to several other parts of the town; and then marched for Salina, where the Saracens fleet lay. On their march, they forcibly took many children from the breasts of their mothers, and flung them on thorns among the hedges, and then stoned them to death.

On the other hand, the Saracens, who had the guard of the king of Cyprus, made him write letters to the admiral of the Christian fleet, containing in substance that he must be careful not to do any damage to the Saracen ships, if he valued the life of the king. Sir Galeran Savary was the bearer of these letters, in a small galliot. The admiral obeyed these orders, which, according to the opinions of many, he ought not to have done; but there was a good deal of fighting between the vessels before these orders arrived, particularly by the bowmen, in which there were very many killed and wounded.

At this affair, Guy, bastard of Burgundy, brother to duke Philip, Simon de Lan, Robert lord de Rebecque, and others from different countries, were made knights, although no vessel was taken on either side, but one having pilgrims on board, as shall be now mentioned. While the fleets were drawing up against each other, a ship, filled with pilgrims eager to acquire honour, concluding for certain that, as the Christian fleet was in sight of the Saracens, a combat must ensue, advanced so near that of the infidels that they could not put back; and notwithstanding succour was instantly sent them, and that they were in sight of the king of Cyprus, they were all hacked to pieces, as butchers would chop meat in a market, excepting a very few who were detained prisoners. Some days after, the Saracen fleet, having the king of Cyprus on board, sailed for Egypt.

On the arrival of the Saracens in Egypt, they conducted the king of Cyprus to Cairo, to the sultan of Babylon, and the other Christian prisoners chained two-and-two like beasts. They dragged after them the banner of the holy Virgin reversed on the ground, and then followed the king mounted on a small mule without saddle, and bound with chains. In this manner were they led into the presence of the sultan of Babylon, and constrained to bow their heads nine times to the very ground, kissing it each time. When they arrived in front of the sultan, who was seated in great pomp in a high gallery, he kept them a full hour in his presence, and then had them conducted to a tower for their prison so long as he should stay in Cairo, where the sultan was served royally and abundantly with all sorts of provision, excepting wine; but this was secretly supplied to him by Christian merchants. The other Cypriot prisoners were confined in divers places.

While the king of Cyprus thus remained prisoner to the sultan of Babylon in Cairo, the archbishop of Nicosia, brother to the king, sent for sir Peter de Lusignan, constable of Jerusalem, and resigned to him the government of the island of Cyprus. He was no sooner in the possession thereof, than he executed rigorous justice by punishing all who, in these times of tribulation, had attempted to revolt. Shortly after, the archbishop returned to Nicosia, which by degrees was repeopled.

In the course of time, a Genoese merchant, named Benedict Percussin, moved by compassion, required of the regency at Cyprus that he might be sent to Cairo, for that he had great hopes of obtaining the king's liberty. He was accordingly sent thither, and was so successful with the sultan that he ransomed the king of Cyprus for two hundred thousand ducats, and on condition that he would also pay an annual tribute to the sultans of Babylon of five thousand ducats. Thus was peace made between the sultan and the king of Cyprus; and on the feast of the Assumption of our Lady, the latter was delivered from chains. After this, the sultan frequently sought opportunities of conversing with him, and put different questions by way of tempting him to abandon the Christian faith; but the king made such sagacious and prudent answers, that the sultan, not knowing how to reply, ordered him refreshments of all sorts, and then dismissed him; for, on the ransom being agreed on, the sultan had him taken from his prison, and lodged in the town.

The king was often permitted to make excursions into the country for his amusement, well mounted, but always attended by some of the Saracens. When part of his ransom was paid, and security accepted for the remainder, on Palm Sunday he had his full liberty, and embarked on board a galley in the port of Alexandria. In company with the admiral of Rhodes, he disembarked at Cerines, where he was met by his sister, his children, and all the nobles and gentlemen of the island, who most reverently and humbly gave thanks to our Lord Jesus Christ for his safe return.

Some days afterward he left Cerines, and went to Nicosia, where he was joyfully received by his subjects, and was lodged at the mansion of the constable of Jerusalem, wherein he ever after remained, because his own palace had been burnt and destroyed by the Saracens. After the death of his queen, Charlotte, he never remarried; nor, as his attendants firmly believed, had he connexion with any other woman: he lived after this for a considerable length of time.

IV. NOTES

1. The main purpose of these notes is to confirm from reliable sources the validity or erroneousness of statements made about Cyprus in Tafur's narrative. In this regard, it is important to establish the dates about which Tafur is writing. The date Tafur began his travels has given rise to much confusion, most of it occasioned, without doubt, by Tafur's lax prose. Jiménez de la Espada writes that Tafur "absented himself from Spain, finally, towards the month of November, perhaps of the year 1435, and he returned between March and April of 1439" (xix). Jiménez attributes his reluctance to fix the year to the fact that Tafur's departure from Spain is an "event related to the siege the second Count Niebla placed around Gibraltar (which cost him his life), and immediately after the rebellion in Genoa against Felipe María Visconti, Duke of Milan, and the defeat of Gaeta by Alfonso V [of Aragon]" (xxv). The siege of Gibraltar and the death of Count Niebla took place in August, 1436; the rebellion in Genoa occurred in December, 1435. Tafur says he went to Genoa after taking part in the siege of Gibraltar; but he also says that he witnessed the rebellion in Genoa in 1435. Consequently, Jiménez concludes that "the two dates turn out to be totally incompatible and a doubt [he] has not yet been able to resolve" (478). However, prominently in the subtitle to his edition, Jiménez decides to date Tafur's voyage between 1435–1439. Letts translates Jiménez' title with these same dates and accepts the reasoning put forward by Jiménez without resolving the doubts (iii, v, 4, 5, 156, 235–6, 246).

José Vives, on the other hand, thinks that he can "fix with absolute certainty that the journey began in the autumn of 1436, one year later than Jiménez supposed," and he chastises Letts for persisting in "the serious error that the journey of Tafur began in 1435" (1938, 146, 130; I cite the 1938 edition always). Vives bases his arguments on the fact that Tafur sees Pope Eugene IV three times, once in Bologna to get the Pope's blessing for the journey to Jerusalem, and twice in Ferrara after returning from Jerusalem. If Tafur's dates cannot be fixed, the Pope's itinerary is a matter of careful record; and there can be no doubt that Tafur received the Pope's blessing in Bologna in 1437. Vives therefore concludes, not quite correctly, as we shall see, that Tafur began his travels in the autumn of 1436. About the discrepancy concerning the rebellion in Genoa in 1435, Vives concludes that since Tafur was writing some 18 years after the event, he might have easily made a mistake, or, he might have made another trip to Genoa (150).

The matter can be resolved, perhaps definitively, if we pay careful attention to Tafur's attempt to state clearly the date his journey began. When Tafur returns to Venice from Constantinople in 1438, he says it was Ascension Day (which fell that year on May 22), he describes the ceremony as the pilgrim ships left Venice for Jerusalem, and he writes, apparently with a clear precise memory, "and on that day and at that hour it was two years since I had left for Jerusalem" (195).

The problem for the major critics (Jiménez, Vives, Letts) has been their assumption that Tafur meant that it had been two years to the day since he had left Venice for Jerusalem; but Tafur does not say "since I had left Venice for Jerusalem," and judging from the date he received the Pope's blessing in 1437, he could not have meant "since I had left Venice." He must, clearly, have meant, "and on that day and at that hour [after hearing Mass] it was two years since I left [home in Spain] for Jerusalem." After leaving his home for Jerusalem, Tafur detained himself to help the Count of Niebla attack Gibraltar. We can safely date the beginning of Tafur's journey from Spain to Jerusalem, therefore, on Ascension Day, May 17, 1436. He left Venice for Jerusalem on Ascension Day, May 9, 1437. On Ascension day, May 22, 1438, Tafur was again in Venice after he had returned from Jerusalem, and he recorded that he had left home exactly two years before. And, about the rebellion in Genoa in 1435, if we are to take Tafur's word that he witnessed it, there being no good reason to doubt him, we must assume that he was in Genoa also in 1435, and had returned to Spain, before he began his journey to Jerusalem.

2. Letts does not say clearly whether he relies solely on Jiménez de la Espada's edition, or whether he also has the eighteenth-century copy before him. His description of the eighteenth-century copy, however, matches Jiménez's language very closely. Vives, writing during the Spanish Civil war, did not know where the eighteenth-century copy was; he later found it in time for the reissue of his monograph in 1947. The manuscript is now housed as MS M-1985 in the library of the University of Salamanca. It is also described by Larkin (4–5), Beaujouan (86), and Marcos (401). I am especially grateful to Professor Carlos Alvar of the University of Alcalá for his help with information about the manuscript and about articles by Rafael Beltrán and José Ochoa Anadón. Professor James B. Larkin has been kind enough to share with me his paleographic transcription of the Cyprus passages of Tafur's narrative and to make suggestions for improving my translation; the remaining errors are mine, not his.

3. The taking of Famagusta by the Genoese is important in Tafur's narrative because it was at Famagusta that the King of Cyprus was crowned King of Jerusalem (Makhairas, 1:309). During the coronation of the young Peter II (age 14) at Famagusta in 1372, a dispute arose between the Genoese and the Venetians about who should hold the right and left reins of the King's horse. The dispute flared up again a few days later at a coronation feast, and the people of Famagusta looted the Genoese shops; many people were killed, and the King blamed the Genoese. Neither the intervention of the Pope nor the mediation of the Knights of Rhodes settled the dispute between the Cypriots and the Genoese. The Genoese declared war after the Cypriots refused to pay the money demanded by the Genoese, and Famagusta was captured by the Genoese in 1374. Young King Peter was held prisoner on the island, but his uncle and the uncle's wife were taken to Mala Paga prison in Genoa. When Tafur writes that the king of Cyprus was taken prisoner in Genoa with his wife, he is wrong in the sense that it was the king's uncle who was taken to Genoa; but Tafur would have been correct had he written "the future king of Cyprus," because Peter's uncle, James, became king in 1382 when Peter died. James's wife, Heloise of Brunswick, did give birth to a son in the Lighthouse Tower at Mala Paga prison, and this son was called Janus after the mythological founder of the city of Genoa. These details are confirmed by Makhairas in the chronicle that covers the period up to the time Tafur visited Cyprus, except that Makhairas makes it clear that Heloise was free to come and go as she pleased, while her husband was confined; so that it is possible that Janus might have been born outside of the prison (Makhairas 1:541; 2:93). Jiménez calls Janus's mother "Inés de Babiera" (462).

4. "And while I was there,": This is the statement, referred to above in note 1, that confuses commentators on Tafur's narrative. The uprising to which Tafur refers took place, according to documents in Genoa and Barcelona, on December 27, 1435 (Vives 148). After this visit in 1435, Tafur must have returned to Castile, from where he left again in 1436 to begin his travels.

5. Perhaps because the name is transcribed in small letters, Letts did not realize it was the name of a jail in Genoa. Dawkins, editor and translator of the chronicle of Makhairas explains: "This prison was called *Mala Paga*, because it was primarily a prison for debtors... Letts in his translation, p. 29, has not noticed that *Mala Paga* is a proper name, and has rendered it by 'the dreadful prison'" (Makhairas 2:187).

6. This is not the only place where the plague hampered Tafur's travels; he cannot visit France for the same reason (257), and he describes pestilence and famine at Sluys (255), and bad air and water on the island of Sardinia (302). A possible reason for the plague to which Tafur refers is given by Makhairas: "And on the twenty-fourth of August 1433 (after Christ), King John de Lusignan was crowned ... And at the same time the wind brought many locusts. And from the beginning of June 1438 after Christ a (great) plague fell upon Lefkosia and the villages, and there were many deaths in all parts of Cyprus; and it lasted seventeen months" (1:681–83). Plagues and rumors of plagues at Cyprus did not always hamper travel there. Sir John Mandeville, travelling roughly one hundred years before Tafur, says that "Cyprus is a very good, fair, and great island,"(Wright 140–41), and he mentions nothing about plagues. In 1480, Felix Fabri, on his first pilgrimage to Jerusalem, stops at Cyprus "for several days, because the master of [the] ship had a brother at Nicosia in the service of the Queen of Cyprus, and had some business to transact with him" (vol. 1, part 1: 23). On the way back, Fabri rode to Nicosia from Salina where the knights travelling with him were admitted by the Queen into the Order of the Kings of Cyprus. When he got back to the galley, Fabri found that two pilgrims had died, and those who went to Nicosia fell ill; but it is not clear that the illnesses were contracted in Cyprus, since the pilgrims arrived weak in Cyprus. By the time Fabri made his second pilgrimage in 1484, his fellow pilgrims insist in the contract that the captain "avoid the kingdom of Cyprus, and not touch there for more than three days, because we have a traditional belief that the air of Cyprus is unwholesome for Germans" (vol. 1, part 1: 87). This stipulation not to stop at Cyprus had become quite common, apparently, around the end of the fifteenth century, and a guidebook for pilgrims to Jerusalem published in England in 1498 bound the captain that he "come not at Famagust in Cyprus for no thing. For many Englishmen and others have died. For that air is so corrupt there about, and the water there also" (Allen 231, 234, 236). Yet, in spite of reports of plague at Cyprus, the Canon Casola survived extended visits to the island during his pilgrimage to Jerusalem in 1494 (Newett 215–19, 293–305, 383–93). Clearly, the plague was not the only hindrance to travel to Cyprus. In 1367, for example, "the Great Council [of Venice] had declared that no pilgrims could go from Venice to Cyprus or Rhodes" because of hostilities between Cyprus and their Venetian allies against the Sultan of Egypt (Newett 29-30). At other times, Cyprus was a necessary stop for Jerusalem, as for example in 1449 when complications with the Sultan of Egypt made travel from Venice to Jerusalem difficult, and pilgrims went to Cyprus from Venice, in search of ships to Jerusalem (Newett 76).

7. By Babylonia, Tafur means Old Cairo, as he himself explains: "in that population there are three districts and all together [as one]; the first they call Greater Babylonia, and the other Cairo, and the other Mistre" (89).

8. The Cardinal was Hugh de Lusignan, Archbishop of Cyprus, elected in 1412 and appointed in 1426; he died in 1442. His brother, whom Tafur calls the "old king," perhaps in the sense of former king, was Janus, born in Genoa in 1374 to James and Heloise of Brunswick, and imprisoned in Cairo in 1426; Janus died of a stroke in 1432 (Hill 3:1088–89).

9. Tafur seems to be mixing famous names here, or his original words have been garbled by copyists. Iolcos was an ancient city in northern Greece, capital of Jason's kingdom. Colchis was the region in Armenia where the golden ram had flown, and where Medea lived. But Tafur is definitely repeating stories here that were told to pilgrims. Makhairas had hoped that the Genoese would lose Famagusta just as the Armenians had lost their castles and towns: "because there are no people more given to faction than the Genoese and the Armenians, both of them cursed folks; for the Armenians had two hundred castles and towns and lost them through (their pride and) factiousness. And this same thing we trust in God will befall this Republic as well" (1:511). In a footnote to this passage by Makhairas, Dawkins cites a reference in *Mandeville's Travels* to an Armenian castle owned by a sorceress who yields her love at the price of constant war in Armenia (Makhairas 2:182–83). About Cypriot claims over Armenia, Amalric's son, Guy de Lusignan, whose mother was an Armenian princess, was the first Cypriot to occupy the Armenian throne in 1342. Guy was assassinated in 1344. Peter I of Cyprus became King of Armenia as well in 1368, but he was assassinated in 1369. His nephew, Leo de Lusignan, was King Leo VI of Armenia in 1374 but was taken captive by the Turks in 1375 and held by them until 1382. When Leo VI died without an heir in 1393, James I of Cyprus claimed the throne of Armenia, and Cypriot kings continued to claim Armenia continuously from that time until Cyprus itself fell to the Venetians in 1489; so that at the time Tafur is writing in 1436, Armenia had been, as he states, part of the kingdom of Cyprus for many years (Hill 2:267–68, 358–59, 380–81, 441–42).

10. Tafur's claim that Nicosia was favored by the king is supported by Nicholas de Martoni, an Italian notary from Carinola who stopped at Cyprus during a pilgrimage to Jerusalem from 1394 to 1395. Martoni wrote that "the said King of Cyprus resides in the said city of Nicosia most of the time since he lost the city of Famagusta" (1, 69–70). Also see Cobham 26.

11. Tafur's claim that Agnes de Lusignan was a spinster and the sister of Janus is supported by Mas Latrie's genealogy and by Dawkins who mentions her briefly: "Agnes is a sister of Janus, who died unmarried" (Makhairas 2:228). Hill relies on Tafur for the claim that Agnes was a close adviser of John II who played a key role in the rebellion to oust James Gurri (2:483, 497). Makhairas says little about her, other than that Cardinal Hugh took her to Kyrenia when he learned that Janus had been taken prisoner by the mamelukes (1:667, 669). About Tafur's guess that she was probably about fifty years old, Agnes is listed by Mas Latrie as younger than Marietta de Lusignan, who was probably born, according to Hill (2:465), around 1380. Marietta died in 1404, but had she lived she would have been about fifty-seven at the time Tafur was describing. This makes Tafur's guess accurate.

12. It might be possible for Cypriot scholars to document Tafur's claim that Hugh de Lusignan was in Italy around 1436 when Tafur left Spain with letters of reference.

13. As a reliable source, Tafur is at a distinct advantage when he writes about Mosen Garcerán Suárez because he spoke to Suárez in Spanish and spent "four or five days" as a guest in Suárez's home in Cyprus. In fact, were it not for Tafur, it would be difficult to identify Suárez, since other sources do not record his name correctly. Makhairas, for example, transcribed the name "Kalserá Souár" (1: 664), and Monstrelet wrote "Gasserant Savari" (Book 2, ch. 39). Tafur also helps us know where Suárez was from, exactly: Makhairas calls him Catalan; Monstrelet calls him "Castelongne," making it easy for some readers to understand "Castilian" and others "Catalan." Tafur clarifies that he was born in Castile, in Segovia; but he also gives him the title "Mosen," which means that he was an Aragonese nobleman; and since the Suárez family is large, Tafur says that this Suárez belonged to the Cernadilla branch. The difference between Catalan and Castilian almost cost Tafur his life in Egypt.

Most of what Tafur says about Suárez can be confirmed from independent sources. Makhairas confirms that Suárez was Admiral of Cyprus (1: 681). Monstrelet confirms that Suárez threw his body between the king and his attackers. Several sources agree that Suárez played an important role in the ransom of the king. The one detail in which Tafur's account differs markedly is in the manner the captive king is treated in Egypt, as Hill explains: "Janus was subjected to degrading treatment. He was made to ride bareback on a lame ass, his feet shackled, barefoot, bareheaded; his banner was reversed and dragged along the ground. He was forced to kiss the ground several times... Pero Tafur, who knew Carceran Suarez, and Loredano are the only writers who conflict with this account...Loredano says that the Sultan received Janus rather favourably, and treated him more as a friend than as a prisoner" (2:486). One way to resolve the conflict is to realize that these passages are culturally loaded with religious overtones. For example, Hill follows Monstrelet in saying that the king's banner was reversed and dragged along the ground, but he leaves out the detail Monstrelet includes, namely that it was "the banner of the Holy Virgin" that was "dragged" and "reversed on the ground." The Virgin Mary is as much revered in Islam as in Christianity, perhaps more in Islam, and it is not likely that an image of her would have been treated as Monstrelet described. Again, despite laws prohibiting Christians from riding horses in Egypt, a Christian King being vilified and made to ride bareback on an ass, as Monstrelet describes, is not degraded but, rather, divinely honored and made to look like Jesus Christ himself. It would be more degrading to have that King ride a horse like a renegade apostate from Christianity, exactly as Tafur describes. In this respect, also, Tafur's account rings verisimilar, especially since Monstrelet includes the detail, ignored by Hill, that the Sultan "frequently sought opportunities of conversing with him, and put different questions by way of tempting him to abandon the Christian faith."

Other minor details in Tafur's version also make sense; for example, that Suárez requested to travel "in Syrian fashion" matches Monstrelet's claim that Suarez was able to save the life of the king by shouting "in the Syrian language, 'It is the king! It is the king!'"; and the detail that the Sultan would accept Suárez's "person" in lieu of a ransom matches the claim made both by Monstrelet and Tafur that Suárez put his "person," his body, between the king and his attackers. In other words, Suárez had made his own person equivalent in value to the king's, because, had it not been for Suárez's body, the Sultan would not have been able to demand ransom for the king.

14. Again, Tafur's account is consistent, and Cypriot scholars ought to be able to confirm it. The fact that Mosen Suárez paid such a key role in negotiating the King's release with the Sultan of Egypt is consistent with the fact that the Sultan's chief interpreter was Spanish, like Suárez; and I would not be surprised if some Cypriot document can be found confirming an annual payment to this interpreter, as Tafur claims. This also explains why the King of Cyprus was willing to use Tafur as a messenger to the Sultan, knowing that Tafur was likely to have as much success with the Sevillian interpreter as Suárez had enjoyed before him.

15. Letts is particularly misleading here. The text says that the king made his daughter, not Suárez, an heir (*e la heredó en su reyno*). Letts mistranslates: "The King also sent for one of his bastard daughters who was there, and married Mosen Suarez to her, and made him his admiral and his heir" (67). The effect seems more or less the same if one is reading casually, but there is a big difference between legitimizing a daughter and placing a male stranger directly in the line of succession. The king realized the wisdom of not doing the latter, especially since he had legitimate sons, as Tafur makes clear.

16. It is interesting that Tafur should mention the sugarcane fields at Damietta and say nothing about them in Cyprus. His mission to the Sultan had a commercial component dealing with taxes on the sale of Cypriot salt in lands controlled by the Sultan. Tafur's interest in sugar, salt, slaves, and islands like Cyprus explains why his contemporaries, like Columbus, would have thought to transfer these commercial paradigms to the islands of the New World. It is a pity that students from the islands of the New World, like the author of this study, were not taught the history of sugar, salt, and slaves in Cyprus.

17. In 1995, I saw a television documentary about the Nile river in which a herd of water buffalo was shown crossing the river as Tafur described. The commentator explained that the crocodiles did not attack the herd because of the noise and fear the water buffalo generated; but the crocodiles would attack lone animals separated from the herd by illness or weakness or inexperience. It is difficult to believe that people could mount one of the crossing wild animals, as Tafur claims he was told, without separating it from the herd. It seems more likely that people would mount their own domesticated water buffalo and cross the river in the safety of the wild herd.

18. Later, Tafur bought three slaves at Kaffa on the Black Sea: "and there I bought two female slaves and one male slave, whom I have today in Cordoba and children from them" (Jiménez 162). Tafur distinguishes himself here from the renegade Jew in Egypt because he says that "Christians have a bull from the Pope to buy them [Christian slaves] and keep them in perpetuity as captives among the Christians of so many nations, so that they do not fall into the hands of Moors and renounce their faith" (Jiménez 162). In other words, Tafur is claiming to be a perfect Christian undoing the damage done to Christians by a renegade Jew from Seville, chief interpreter to the Sultan of Egypt.

Ironically, Rafael Ramírez de Arellano (289-93), the scholar who has discovered more documents about the Tafur family than anyone else, suspects reluctantly that Tafur might have behaved exactly as the renegade Jew from Seville, and that a mysterious woman called Brianda Tafur who inherited a house and money from Tafur and was named in the will drawn up by Tafur's wife might, in fact, have been a daughter of Pero Tafur by one of the slaves he bought in Kaffa.

Another possibility, of course, is that Tafur took the Papal Bull seriously and meant to keep those slaves in perpetuity. Since he admits having the slaves and their children with him in Cordoba as he writes, Brianda might not necessarily be his child at all but one of the female slaves he bought when she was young (18, for example) in 1438 (the will is dated 1490); or, Brianda Tafur might be her illegitimate child, if the female slave he bought carried the Tafur family name. It was not uncommon for slaves to carry their master's surname; and it was common for Jewish slaveowners, especially, to leave substantial inheritances to their most faithful slaves. Tafur's wife says that what she wills to Brianda Tafur is "for services that she has done and does every day" for her (Ramírez de Arellano 289–91).

There are other possibilities that some document now unknown will confirm or deny. For example, Vives (132) thinks that Tafur may have been married twice. This means, if it were true, that Brianda might have been a daughter by Tafur's first wife, who had died. Ramírez discards this possibility because, unlike most other people mentioned in the documents he found, Brianda's relationship to the person writing is not stated; if she were a legitimate daughter, or a servant, or even a slave, Ramírez reasons, the document would have said so.

19. It is inconceivable that any Spaniard reading this passage by Tafur in the fifteenth century would not have compared what Tafur describes as forced conversion in Egypt with forced conversion in Spain at the same time. In Egypt, Tafur explains, forced converts are exalted; in Spain they are persecuted. The double indictment would have been clear to any Spanish Jew or converso: both Christianity and Islam use forced conversion, in Tafur's words, to "augment their religion"; Jews might proselytize among backsliding Jews and even, as in the famous case of Saul (Acts 9.1,2), persecute renegade Jews; but forced conversion is unknown in Judaism. The same verb "augment" was used by a Spanish converso writer after Tafur: Jorge de Montemayor described conversos in Spain who are used by Inquisitors to "augment the holy Catholic faith on earth" (Nepaulsingh 1995, 113–14).

20. Jiménez (575) defines the *rótulo* as an Egyptian pound equivalent to 18 Castilian ounces.

21. Tafur probably means to justify his clever lying to Conti at first because Conti is dressed as a converted Moor. He tells Conti the whole truth only after he is assured that Conti is a Christian forced to convert to Islam and intending to revert to Christianity at the earliest convenient opportunity. Conti did return to Catholicism, and as penance, the Pope ordered him to tell his story to the papal secretary, Poggio Bracciolini. For a detailed comparison of what Conti said to Tafur and later to Poggio, see Vives 176–190.

22. Mas Latrie (1882, 76–82) cites Tafur in his account of Cardinal Hugh of Lusignan, but he makes no mention of this bishop of Paphos who died when Tafur returned to Cyprus. Makhairas (1: 673, 683) mentions a Latin bishop (of Paphos?) called Brother Solomon who was robbed by the soldiers of King Alexis. Cypriot scholars can probably determine the validity of Tafur's claim that the Bishop of Paphos died in 1437.

23. This is the same James Gurri whom Tafur identifies earlier as being sent to Castile to raise ransom money to pay for the release of King Janus of Cyprus when the

King was taken captive to the Sultan of Egypt's court. After King Janus died, James Gurri was appointed to the Council of forty people who advised the young King John. By coincidence this King John was John II of Cyprus at a time when Castile also had a King John II who had recommended Tafur's travels. By coincidence also, Castile's King John II was, like his namesake in Cyprus, a minor. By further coincidence, Alvaro de Luna in Castile was a royal favorite whose access to the king also caused powerful nobles to attack the king and his favorite repeatedly, especially in 1441 when Alvaro de Luna was exiled for six years. It would be impossible, therefore, for readers in Castile not to have drawn parallels between what Tafur related about Cyprus in 1437 and similar incidents in Castile in 1441.

James Gurri was also a favorite of Queen Helena, the Greek wife of King John II of Cyprus. John II and Helena had a daughter, Charlotte, whose husband died suddenly and mysteriously. John II also had an illegitimate son, James the Bastard who later became James II of Cyprus. Charlotte complained to James the Bastard that her mother, Queen Helena, was implicated in the mysterious death of Charlotte's husband. James the Bastard killed Queen Helena's brother, the chamberlain; and James the Bastard was forced to escape from Cyprus for this act of revenge. James the Bastard blamed James Gurri, Queen Helena's partisan, for forcing him to escape from Cyprus, and soon the Bastard returned to Cyprus and murdered Gurri in 1457.

When James the Bastard escaped from Cyprus he left in a caravel owned by a John Tafur, and apparently this John Tafur helped James the Bastard murder Gurri. For his loyalty to James the Bastard, John Tafur was made Count of Tripoli and captain of Famagusta (Hill 2:488, 3:497, 537–39; Mas Latrie 1882, 84–89).

We know that Pero Tafur had a son named Juan, and other members of Tafur's family were named Juan (Ramírez de Arellano 284–88). It seems more than coincidental that a John Tafur should begin to figure prominently in the history of Cyprus shortly after Pero Tafur was on the island in 1437. Cypriot scholars ought to be able to determine whether or not John Tafur, Count of Tripoli, was a relative of Pero Tafur.

Tafur is aware that his surname refers pejoratively in Spanish to card-sharpers who swindle in card games. This is probably why he describes the Turks, on his visit to Adrianopolis as "a noble people in whom much truth is found, and they live in that land as noblemen as much in their expenditures as in their finery and cuisine and games, for they are very clever (*tahures*), a very happy people and very humane and well-spoken, so much so that in those parts, when virtue is spoken of, it is not with reference to any other than to the Turks" (Jiménez 156). In this passage Tafur uses the word *tahures* in a virtuous context, reversing the pejorative connotation of "clever" in the sense of cheating. The passage is therefore to be linked to the one where Tafur's life is at risk in the Governor's house in Egypt, while Tafur was on his way to see the Sultan: "And while I was there some Moors came saying that I was Catalan, that they had seen me eat with the Lord of Candelor, and that they wanted to prove it. And they brought two Turks, pagan nobles who were there, so that they could tell the truth. And they came to me and looked at me and said that the Moors were lying. And I asked, 'If the Turks had said otherwise, what would have become of me?' And they said death, that whatever the Turks say is approved as truth" (fol. 24v: 10–15, and my translation above, p. 13). Tafur's narrative reflects a kind of cleverness that shows that the author was intent on restoring nobility to the meaning of his name. Tafur may not have been unaware that the Hebrew Bible uses the consonants in his name (*thr*) repeatedly to form a root word meaning "clean, pure, fair" (see, for example, Exodus 25.11, Leviticus 13.6, Zechariah 3.5).

24. It is very likely that the king of Cyprus offered a leopard to Tafur, because contemporary accounts document the long-standing tradition in Cyprus of hunting with leopards. Martoni (70), for example, wrote that the King of Cyprus "holds great state especially in hunting, for he himself owns twenty-four leopards and three hundred hawks of all species, some of which he carries every day to the hunt" (slightly different translation by Home 60). And a German priest wrote that "there are in Cyprus wild rams [moufflon] which are not found in other parts of the world. But they are caught with leopards, in no other way can they be taken" (Home 60; see also Cobham 20, 21).

25. These marriage proposals are probably why Tafur, knowing that the King of Cyprus was marriageable, suggested that the Sultan of Egypt's Chief Interpreter would have done better to send the Cypriot king a daughter of the Governor of Damietta rather than a crocodile skin (my translation above, p. 19).

26. Tafur's description of King Janus's physique is not at odds with the portrait found in Hill (2:447): "He is described by the chroniclers as tall and fat, physically strong, good-looking, with a slight blond beard... He was too heavy for the second horse he rode at Khirokitia."

27. Tafur's association of the name Kyrenia with Achilles can be documented in other contemporary sources: "Caumont, A.D. 1418, reports the contemporary opinion that it was built by Achilles" (Makhairas 2:173). The medieval fortress at Kyrenia was difficult to capture; Makhairas gives a detailed account of an attempt by the Genoese to capture Kyrenia in 1374 (1:453–517); Makhairas also confirms Tafur's claim that Lady Agnes and other members of the royal court of Cyprus went to Kyrenia when the Moslems attacked Cyprus in 1426 and took King Janus hostage to Egypt (Makhairas 1:667–68). Hill (2:19, n.3) gives the etymology of the name, justifying Tafur's spelling "Aherines": "The name of the place ... in the older western writers shows that the Greek initial guttural had been palatalized, for from the beginning they generally call it Cerines or Cherines and the like ... Leake gives Gherne as the Turkish name ... It is now Girne."

28. "Meridional," that is, from the region of midday from the south. Tafur is playing on the words "midnight" and "midday" here, because *mediodia*, in Spanish, means both midday and south.

29. Tafur had mentioned (my translation above, p. 21) that the saltponds at Castelrosso brought good income to Rhodes, and part of Tafur's mission to the Sultan of Egypt involved the sale of salt in Syria tax-free (my translation above, p. 17). This revenue from the sale of salt might have been the subject of the letters Tafur carried to the Grand Master; cf. Jiménez (451) who thinks that the letters Tafur carried might have had to do with the sale of land which the Grandmaster of Rhodes wanted to buy from the King of Cyprus.

30. According to Jiménez (449–52, 581), this Grandmaster of Rhodes was the Catalan, Antón de Fluvián, who died on October 29, 1437.

BIBLIOGRAPHY

Allen, P. S. *The Age of Erasmus*. New York: Russell & Russell, 1963.

Badía Margarit, A. M. "Hungría vista por Pero Tafur, viajero español del siglo XV." In *Mélanges de linguistique et de littérature romanes a la mémoire d'Istvan Frank*, 31–38. Saarbrücken: Universität des Saarlandes, 1957.

Baer, Yitzhak. *A History of the Jews in Christian Spain*. 2 vols. Philadelphia: The Jewish Publication Society of America, 1961.

Beaujouan, G. *Manuscrits scientifiques médiévaux de l'Université de Salamanque et de ses 'colegios mayores.'* Bordeaux: Bibliothèques de l'École des Hautes Études Hispaniques, 1962.

Beltrán, Rafael. "Tres itinerarios trazados sobre el *Tratado de las andanças e viajes de Pero Tafur.*" *Monteolivete* (1985): 17–34.

———. "Sobre el género de *tratado* de Pero Tafur: entre el libro de viajes y la autobiografía." In *Actas del II Congreso de la Asociación hispánica de literatura medieval, 1987*, 203–215. Alcalá: Universidad de Alcalá, 1992.

Bibliography of Old Spanish Texts, BOOST, see Faulhaber.

Bravo García, Antonio. "La Constantinopla que vieron R. González de Clavijo y Pero Tafur: los monasterios." *Erytheia* 2 (1983): 39–47.

Cobham, C. D. *Excerpta Cypria*. Cambridge: Cambridge University Press, 1908.

Dawkins, R. M., ed. and trans. *Recital Concerning the Sweet Land of Cyprus Entitled 'Chronicle,'* by Leontios Makhairas. 2 vols. Oxford: Clarendon, 1932

Deyermond, A. D. "La voz personal en la prosa hispánica medieval." In *Actas del X congreso de la asociación internacional de hispanistas (1989)*, 161–170. Barcelona: PPU, 1992.

Fabri, Felix. *The Book of the Wanderings of Brother Felix Fabri*. Trans. Aubrey Stewart. London: Hanover Square, vol. 1, part 1, 1892, vol. 1, part 2, 1893, vol. 2, part 1, 1897, vol. 2, part 2, 1897. This four-volume translation is part of the Palestine Pilgrims' Text Society series, vols. 7, 8, 9, and 10. See also Cobham 36–47.

Faulhaber, Charles B. et al., eds. *Bibliography of Old Spanish Texts*, 3rd ed. Madison, Wisconsin: Seminary of Medieval Studies, 1984.

González de Clavijo, Ruy. *Embajada a Tamorlán*. Ed. Francisco López Estrada. Madrid: Nueva Colección de Libros Raros o Curiosos, 1943.

González Llubera, Ignacio. *Viajes de Benjamín de Tudela*. Madrid: Sanz Calleja, 1918.

Hill, Sir George. *A History of Cyprus*. 3 vols. Cambridge: Cambridge University Press, 1948.

Home, Gordon. *Cyprus Then and Now*. London: Dent, 1960.

Jiménez de la Espada, Marcos, ed. *Andanças e viajes de un hidalgo de España*. Barcelona: Albir, 1982.

———, ed. *Andanças é viajes de Pero Tafur por diversas partes del mundo avidos*. Madrid: Miguel Ginesta, 1874.

Johnes, Thomas, trans. *The Chronicles of Enguerrand de Monstrelet*. London: William Smith, 1845.

Labarge, Margaret Wade. "Pero Tafur: A Fifteenth Century Spaniard." *Florilegium* 5 (1983): 237–247.

Larkin, James Brian. *A Morphological and Syntactical Study of Fifteenth-Century Spanish Prose*. Ph.D. Diss. Stanford University, 1965.

Letts, Malcolm, ed. and trans. *Pero Tafur: Travels and Adventures 1435-1439*. New York: Harper, 1926.

Luke, Sir Harry. *Cyprus*. London: Harrap, 1957.

López Estrada, Francisco, ed., see Jiménez de la Espada 1982.

Loredano, Gianfrancesco. *Histoire des rois de Chypre de la maison de Lusignan*. Traduit de l'Italien du Cavalier Henri Giblet Cypriot. 2 vols. Paris: André Cailleau, 1732.

Makhairas, Leontios, see Dawkins.

Marcos Rodríguez, F. "Los manuscritos pretridentinos hispanos de ciencias sagradas en la Biblioteca Universitaria de Salamanca." *Repertorio de Historia de las Ciencias Eclesiásticas en España* 2 (1971).

Martoni, Nicolas de. *Relation du Pelerinage a Jerusalem*. Paris: Leroux, 1895. See also Cobham 22–28.

Mas Latrie, Louis de. *Histoire de l'île de Chypre sous le règne des princes de la maison de Lusignan*. 3 vols. Paris: l'Imprimerie Imperiale, 1852–55, 1861.

——. *Histoire des archevêques latins de l'île de Chypre*. Genes: l'Institut Royal des Sourds-Muets, 1882.

Monstrelet, Enguerran de. *Chroniques*. Paris: Renouard, 1860; rpt. New York: Johnson Reprint Corporation, 1966.

Monstrelet, Enguerrand de. *The Chronicles*. See Johnes, Thomas.

Nepaulsingh, Colbert I. *Towards a History of Literary Composition in Medieval Spain*. Toronto: University of Toronto Press, 1987.

——. *Apples of Gold in Filigrees of Silver: Jewish Writing in the Eye of the Spanish Inquisition*. New York: Holmes and Meier, 1995.

Newett, Margaret M. *Canon Pietro Casola's Pilgrimage to Jerusalem in the Year 1494*. Manchester: Manchester University Press, 1907.

Ochoa Anadón, José. "Pero Tafur: un hidalgo español emparentado con el emperador bizantino. Problemas de heráldica." *Erytheia* 6 (1985): 283–293.

——. "El viaje de Tafur por las costas griegas." *Erytheia* 8 (1987): 33–62.

——. "El viaje de Pero Tafur por Tierra Santa." In *Actas del II congreso de la asociación hispánica de literatura medieval (1987)*. Alcalá: University of Alcalá, 1992.

Peters, F. E. *Jerusalem*. Princeton: Princeton University Press, 1985.

Ramírez de Arellano, Rafael. "Estudios biográficos: Pero Tafur." *Boletín de la Real Academia de la Historia*. 41 (1902): 273–293.

Round, Nicholas G. *The Greatest Man Uncrowned*. London: Tamesis, 1986.

Tafur, Pero. See Cobham (31–34), Letts, Jiménez de la Espala.

Tudela, Benjamín de. See González Llubera, Ignacio, and Wright, Thomas.

Vasiliev, A. "Pero Tafur, A Spanish Traveler of the Fifteenth Century and his Visit to Constantinople, Trebizond, and Italy." *Byzantion* 7 (1932): 74–122.

———. "A Note on Pero Tafur." *Byzantion* 10 (1935): 65–66.

Vives, José. "Andanças e Viajes de un hidalgo español." In *Gesammelte Aufsätze Zur Kulturgeschichte Spaniens*, ed. H. Finke. Münster: Aschendorffsche, 1938. I cite this edition always.

———. *Andanças e viajes de un hidalgo español (Pero Tafur 1436–39)*. Barcelona: Balmesiana, 1947; also included in Jiménez de la Espada 1982.

Wright, Thomas, ed. *Early Travels in Palestine*. 1848, rpt. New York: KTAV, 1968.

INDEX

—A—

Achilles, 20, 61
Adrianopolis, 22, 60
Agnes, Lady, 11, 12, 19, 20, 38, 40, 56, 61
Aherines [Kyrenia], 20, 61
Alexandria, 15, 18, 19, 32, 52
Antioch, 11, 25
Armenia, 10, 11, 21, 24, 25, 41, 56
Ascension Day, 10, 53, 54

—B—

Babylonia [Old Cairo], 10, 12, 13, 18, 24–29, 31, 32, 35–37, 56
Baffa [Paphos], 50
Beaulieu (near Limassol), 48
Beirut, 11
Benjamin of Tudela, 8
berets, 4
Bologna, 9, 22, 53

—C—

Cairo, 10, 18, 51, 56
Castelrosso, 10, 21, 41, 61
Castile, 4–8, 12, 20, 55, 57, 59
    king of, 4
Castilians, 5, 7, 8
Catholics, Catholicism, 5, 59
Cerines [Kyrenia], 50, 52, 61
Charlotte, 47, 52, 60
Cherines [Kyrenia], 61
Chios, 9
Christians, Christianity, 3, 5–8, 15, 16, 18, 22, 49, 50, 57–59
Citolye, 48, 49
cockatrice, 14, 19, 61
Colchis, 56
Columbus, 8

Constantinople, 3–7, 21, 22, 53, 64
Conti, Niccolo, 5, 7, 18, 59
converso, 5–7, 59
Córdoba, 6, 8
Cyprus
    Cardinal of, 1, 10, 13, 17, 22, 38, 56
    health conditions, 10, 11, 20, 55
    King of, 1, 3, 9, 11–13, 15, 17–19, 21, 22, 54
    misrule, 3, 4
    Order of the Kings, 55
    plague, 10, 55
    Queen of, 55

—D—

Damietta, 13, 19, 29, 31, 58, 61
Dawkins, R. M., 55, 56, 62, 63
Domy, 49

—E—

Egypt, 1, 3–7, 10, 11, 17, 22, 51, 55, 57–61

—F—

Fabri, Felix, 55, 62
Famagusta, 3, 9, 11, 54, 56, 60
Florence, 3, 4, 9, 22

—G—

Genoa, 3, 9, 11, 53, 54–56
Germany, 4
    Duke of, 20
Gherne [Kyrenia], 61
Gibraltar, 6, 7, 9, 53, 54
Girne [Kyrenia], 61
Gostanza, 11, 25
Guiri, Jacobo [James Gurri], 8, 12, 19, 27, 38, 56, 59, 60

—H—

Hebrew (Biblical), 7, 61
Helena, Queen of King John II, 60
Heloise of Brunswick, Queen of James I, 54, 56
Henry III, king of Castile, 8
Hill, Sir George, 56, 57, 60, 61, 63
Hugh de Lusignan, 56, 57

—I—

India, 8, 18, 37
Iolcos, 56
Islam, 16, 17, 57, 59

—J—

Jaffa, 10, 11
James I, King of Cyprus, 54, 56, 60
James II, King of Cyprus (the Bastard), 60
Janus, King of Cyprus, 9, 11, 20, 23, 26, 43, 54, 56, 57, 59, 61
    birth, 9
    death, 56
    description of, 20, 61
    in battle of Khirokitia, 48-53
Jerusalem, 1, 3, 4, 5, 8–11, 15, 19, 37, 49, 51–56, 63, 64
Jews, Judaism, 5–8, 12, 15, 58, 59, 62, 64
Jiménez de la Espada, Marcos, 2, 53, 54, 63, 65
John I, King of Castile, 5
John II, King of Spain, 12
John II, King of Cyprus, 1, 7, 55
Juan II, King of Castile, 7
Juana de Horozco, wife of Tafur, 6

—K—

Khirokitia, 61
    battle of, 48-53
Kyrenia, 20, 56, 61

—L—

Larkin, James B., 2, 8, 23, 54, 63
Lefkosia [Nicosia], 55
leopard, 20, 61
Letts, Malcolm, 1–3, 53–55, 58, 63, 64
locusts, 55
Loredano, 57, 63
Luna, Alvaro de, 7, 8, 60
Lymeson [Limassol], 48

—M—

Madrid, 2, 5, 63
Makhairas, 54–57, 59, 61–63
Mala Paga prison, 9, 54, 55
mameluke, 3, 16, 17, 56
Mandeville, Sir John, 55, 56
Medea, 11
Milan, 4
    duke of, 9
Monstrelet, Enguerrand de, 23, 43, 48, 57, 63, 64
Moors, 4, 6–9, 12, 13, 18, 20, 58, 60
Moslems, 22, 61
mosque, 16
moufflon, 61
Mytilene, 9

—N—

Nicosia, 11, 19, 25, 26, 38, 40, 48, 50–52, 55, 56
    Citadel, 19, 38
    royal palace, 50
    Saint George, church of, 11
Niebla, Count, 7, 9, 53, 54
Nile, 13, 14, 29, 58
Noah's Ark, 11

—P—

Palestine, 5, 62, 65
Paphos, 10, 13, 19, 59
Pedro de la Randa, 7, 18, 19
Peter I, King of Cyprus, 54, 56
Peter II, King of Cyprus, 54
Pifani, Saint, cape of, 20, 40

pigeons (carrier), 13
Pisa, 4, 9, 22
plague, 10, 13, 21, 55
Pope, 7, 12, 21, 53, 54, 58, 59
Prester John, 8, 18

—Q—

quails, 14

—R—

Ramírez de Arellano, Rafael, 6, 58–60
Rhodes, 10, 20, 21
    Order of, 1, 10, 20, 21, 54, 61
Rome, 5, 6, 9

—S—

Salina [Larnaca], 50, 55
salt, 17, 21, 41, 58, 61
Saracens, 48–52
Saul [Paul the Apostle], 59
Savoy
    Duke of, 20
Seville, 5, 7, 12, 15, 58
Sinai, Mount, 6, 10, 12, 13, 17, 18
slaves, 3, 4, 7, 58, 59
sodomy, 8, 10
Spain, 1, 4–6, 8, 12, 16, 18, 22, 53, 54, 57, 59, 62, 64
Suárez, Mosen, 7, 12, 28, 57, 58
sugarcane, 13, 58
Sultan of Egypt, 1, 3–5, 7, 10–13, 18, 19, 33, 35, 36, 55, 57, 58, 60, 61
Susan, island, 6
synagogue, 5, 6
Syria, 11, 49, 57, 61

—T—

Tafur, Brianda, 58, 59
Tafur, John, 60
Tafur, Pero
    birth, 5
    composition of narrative, 3, 4, 8
    date of composition, 53
    date of travels, 1, 53–55
    editions, 2
    his ancestry, 3–7, 21, 58
    his daughter, 58
    his name, 7, 60
    his prose, 1
    his religion, 5–7
    his sister, 6
    his son, 60
    his wife, 6, 59
    in Cyprus, 3, 9-13, 19-21
    in Egypt, 13-17
    in Venice, 22
    literary purpose, 3
    manuscript, 2, 22, 54
    narrative, 53, 54
    paragraph divisions, 1–11, 18, 19, 21–23, 53–65
    translations, 1, 53
    travels, 3, 4, 9, 22
tahur, 7
tahures, 60
Tamburlaine, 8
taxes, 7, 17, 58, 61
Thenorio, Diego, 13, 28
Toledo, 5
Turkey, 8, 10, 20
Turks, 3, 4, 5, 13, 20, 56, 60

—V—

Venice, 1, 3–6, 9, 22, 53, 55
Vives, Jose, 53–55, 59, 65

—W—

water-buffalo, 14
weasels, 13
women, status of, 15, 16

—Y—

Yllan, Pedro, 3, 6